BECOMING SUSAN

Finding joy and delight, fulfilment and
purpose, fun and meaning in life again

SUSAN HOLT

Becoming Susan: Finding joy and delight, fulfilment and purpose, fun and meaning in life again
© Susie Holt 2023

ISBN: 978-1-922956-67-5 (paperback)
         978-1-922956-68-2 (eBook)

A catalogue record for this book is available from the National Library of Australia

Printed in Australia by Ocean Reeve Publishing
www.oceanreevepublishing.com
Published by Susie Holt and Ocean Reeve Publishing

REEVE
PUBLISHING

DISCLAIMER

This story may have some information that triggers self-confidence issues. Each person is an individual and the self-help techniques and questions that are posed at the end of each chapter are prompters only.

If you are feeling desperate or depressed, seek professional help. Remember, you are not alone …

DEDICATION

This labour of love is dedicated to the constant loves of my life.

To my parents, Alan and Marilyn. Thank you for always supporting the weird twists and turns my life has taken.

To my sister, Cathy. Thank you for being there for me at all times. I can't imagine my life without you.

To my husband, Luke, and my sons, Tyson, Royden, and Toby. I can't imagine my life without you, though I imagine that, without you, I wouldn't have nearly so many stories to tell and I might have finished this book two years earlier! Thanks for making space for me to figure out the best way to be me.

CONTENTS

INTRODUCTION

I had a conversation recently that really challenged me.

I'm a working mum. I have a good job doing a fun talk show on radio, syndicated across Australia, with my husband where we laugh a lot. We've worked together on radio since 2007. I love my family—a loving husband and three fun-loving, affectionate, kind, rambunctious sons. I love where I live on the Gold Coast in Queensland, Australia, with the beach and mountains nearby and the weather that draws tourists all year-round. Yet, in the midst of it all, I feel like something is missing. I can't quite put my finger on it. Maybe it's fulfilment. Maybe it's a sense of purpose. Maybe it's just the constant longing for more.

The conversation I had was about how mums can often lose confidence after having children, despite having had successful careers. Intelligent, driven women lose that sense of clarity and wholeness. For me, that resonated and made sense of how I've been feeling for all too long now.

I wouldn't change becoming a mum for anything, but I did lose that sense of self and drive to live a life that I get to design, choosing instead to take only those opportunities that come to me. Summing it up, I feel that I've had a personal identity crisis.

My life has been designed by chance and not with a clear, consistent, passionate purpose, and it's time to take back control.

So, now it's time to take life back to a place where I feel that feeling—the one where I'm okay with me ... living purposefully with fulfilment.

The biggest challenge I have is remembering the little lessons along the way in life that point the way. I've been privileged to speak to many experts who specialise in mental health, wellbeing, and helping others find their purpose in life. This book is a journey through some life lessons that I've discovered along the way, and some I've drawn from the wisdom of those around me, all in a bid to create a roadmap back to me.

Will you join me in moving towards a life that fills you with joy and delight, fulfilment and purpose, fun and meaning?

Chapter 1:

JUST DO IT

Somewhere along the way, I've started to become aware that *the thing I don't want to do is all too often the thing that makes me feel the best.*

Isn't that just the worst? I mean, I'd like a life where I always want to do the things that are best for me and those around me and where I don't want to do the wrong things.

Unfortunately, that's not how the dreaded 'comfort zone' works.

I don't think it's possible to count the number of times I've relearnt this lesson in my life.

I'd love to be the kind of person who learns something and implements it in their life and that's that. Unfortunately, I'm more of a 'learn it, do it for a bit, and then forget it' kind of gal. For this idea to sink in, I have to relearn it frequently, because when there's something I don't want to do, I'm good at convincing myself to not do it. It's one of the great privileges of adulthood to have the choice. Sometimes, I think I'd do a whole lot better in life if someone else just told me what to do, but then that would require me to be more consistently obedient than I probably am.

When it comes to the things we don't necessarily *want* to do, there's the list that is pretty common—exercise, healthy eating, cleaning, and washing. Then there are the opportunities that are presented that make us feel uncomfortable with the thoughts that we're not the right person, or we're not skilled enough, or we'll fail if we try. These are the times when we want to say no purely out of fear. Yet, I have found out the hard way that saying yes when we want to say no in both the big and the little things can stretch our capacity, bring a sense of order and peace, and ultimately, create a pathway to fulfilment.

During the lockdown of the COVID pandemic, a friend of mine reached out and we started walking, once a week, on a Friday morning. We'd meet at 6 am, grab a coffee, and walk for several kilometres. It wasn't fast, but we'd talk the whole way, and I'd always feel amazing by the time I got home. I looked forward to it as a highlight of every week.

Once the lockdown lifted and life returned to a semblance of normality, both of our routines changed, and we couldn't meet any more. The result was that, bit by bit, week by week, I was walking less and less until I stopped walking with any kind of regularity.

I'd been seeing a female psychologist for a while, having recognised that stress, anxiety, and depression were rearing their ugly heads in my life. In one of our sessions, I talked about knowing how good walking had made me feel every day, but now, I just wasn't doing it. At no point did my psychologist give me a solution. Then I realised, it was because the solution was obvious. The way to get up and go walking in the morning is … to get up and go walking in the morning.

My current reality is that I love baked goods, I don't like exercise, and I'm hit-and-miss on cleaning. Consequently, my weight is higher than ideal, my energy is lower than desired, and my house is, well, inconsistent in tidiness. When I'm in the zone, I'm great at getting it done. I can exercise like a machine, clean like a machine, and eat like someone who eats really well. I'm just not very consistent about being in the zone.

On our radio show, Luke, my co-host—who happens to be my husband—and I spoke with Kate Christie, director and founder of Time Stylers, about changing your life in ninety seconds.[1] The first few seconds are for identifying the goal, the next few seconds are for identifying the barriers, the next are for determining your values, the next for creating a visual image example of what the goal looks like when it's achieved, and the final few seconds are used to determine the first action step. I think the biggest part of this process is recognising that the things we often want to say no to are actually the things that align well with our values. When we can see the purpose in the action as it aligns with our values, moving from a no to a yes seems easier (not necessarily easy) and also logical.

As an example of putting this process into action, let's take losing weight.

Step 1: What is the goal? To feel less self-conscious, more comfortable in clothes, healthier, and more energetic.

Step 2: What are the barriers? I love processed/sugar-filled/fried food, and I feel exhausted and overwhelmed all the time. Sometimes, I battle a 'what's the point?' kind of attitude.

---

[1] Time Stylers (2023), *About Kate Christie*, viewed from <https://www.timestylers.com/about/>.

Step 3: What do I value? My most relevant value here is family and health. I want to be able to have fun and energy with my young boys and I want to feel good in my body.

Step 4: What does this goal look like when applied to my life? For example, in the summer of (insert appropriate year here!) I will run and play on the beach with my boys and our dog and feel confident in a swimsuit so that I can jump in the water with them.

Step 5: What is the first action step? Move a little more every day as measured by the number of steps that I take. (Remember, this is just a first step. We don't need to plan out the whole solution here.)

Like most people, if I think too long about something, I'm very capable of finding a reason not to do it. A simple process that can be walked through in a few seconds, like the steps above, can create a clear path to the ultimate goal that is based on living according to my values as opposed to giving in to my fears. *Joy and delight, fulfilment and purpose, fun and meaning, are my personal goals.*

Let me backtrack a bit. Back at school, and then when I started university, I studied computer science as a subject and spent a whole lot of time on 'if, then, else'. If x happens, then do y, else do z. I feel like this kind of thinking process, if coded correctly, could serve in turning the right noes into yeses. For example, if I think I should go for a walk, then I should create the opportunity for me to go for a walk, else I am robbed of the energy and health benefits it provides.

By the way, the only reason I studied computer science for a short time is that university study showed up some fundamental failings in my ability to study, even though I'd done well academically at school. Mostly, it was this whole problem that presented itself way back then. I was very good at choosing fun, friends, and frivolity over study and, to be honest, sometimes even showing up to class in the first place was an issue.

One day, I decided it was time to finally do the assignment that was due for computer science and, not owning my own computer at that point—back in the day before smartphones, tablets, and affordable laptops—I headed off to the computer labs to do my work. I walked in to find the room about three-quarters full of students but quickly found a free Apple Mac to sit down at. I pulled out the criteria for the assessment that we had to do, turned on the machine, and stared at the screen. *Login*—it was asking for a username and password. I stared blankly at the screen for a bit, while my brain raced at a cracking pace, confusing itself trying to remember back to class one. After a couple of minutes, I stood up and walked out.

I was pretty sure that being able to log into a computer was a critical skill for succeeding in the subject, so I walked myself off to the dean's office and said farewell to computer science. I decided to change to an arts degree majoring in psychology. In short, I'm looking forward to about ten years when I call my children with an immediate technical need and an extensive lack of skill on my end to fulfil it. I expect the call will be filled with me repeatedly saying, 'What do you mean?' and, 'My computer doesn't have that button.'

If I'd done the things I didn't want to do, like attend class and do the weekly tasks they assigned us, I could have avoided this whole situation and probably, somewhere along the way, would have had an inner glow of fulfilment from, you know, actively participating in my own tertiary education.

Needless to say, getting this lesson straight in my life has been a long time coming.

At this point, I feel it's important to get something really clear. This isn't about feeling guilty for not learning lessons earlier, younger, or sooner. Along the way, I could equally recount stories of times when success has come my way because I did do the hard thing that I didn't want to do, or didn't feel like doing, and was rewarded with the feeling of fulfilment. This experience is about saying that, for me, now is the time to take life to a level when I allow myself to feel the good things more often and more deeply. *The stories of failing are the anecdotes of richness that are the stepping stones to appreciating the stories of winning.* They let me recognise my own shortcomings. They give me cause to laugh at myself. They let me appreciate the journey of my children more because I don't expect them to learn every lesson right away—I demonstrably haven't. I just hope it doesn't take them as long.

So, here's the takeaway for lesson one: In order to do the things that I don't want to do that make me feel best, I need to have a clear process for determining what is a yes and what is a no that is based on my personal values and goals of joy and delight, fulfilment and purpose, fun and meaning.

Life Lesson: Don't let fear determine your yes and your no.

Takeaway: In order to do the things that I don't want to do that make me feel best, I need to have a clear process for determining what is a yes and what is a no that is based on my personal values and goals of joy and delight, fulfilment and purpose, fun and meaning.

Questions:

- What are your personal values to help determine a yes from a no in your life?
- What are your personal goals?
- When was there a time in your life when saying yes to something that was difficult turned out to be a good decision (even though it took you out of your comfort zone)?

Chapter 2:

CLEAN SHEETS AND FRESH PYJAMAS

You've probably come across the Serenity Prayer, normally attributed to Dr Reinhold Niebuhr.[2] I remember seeing it for the first time in a little Christian bookstore in Caboolture, Australia, where I grew up. 'God, grant me the serenity to accept the things I cannot change, courage to change the things I can, and wisdom to know the difference.'

There have been a lot of times when I've failed on all three counts of the Serenity Prayer. I've not accepted circumstances out of my control, I've not had the courage to change things I could, and I haven't had the wisdom to always know what I can and cannot change. The easiest thing would be to think of *myself* as something that can't change. Then, I could determine not to resent myself and we could call it a day. Phew! Problem solved.

---

[2] AA Grapevine (1964), *The Serenity Prayer*, viewed from <https://www.aagrapevine.org/magazine/1964/nov/serenity-prayer> and <https://quoteinvestigator.com/2019/12/24/serenity/>.

Unfortunately, there's too much evidence to suggest I can change, given that I own a smartphone, in spite of my earlier confession of a lack of technical skill, and I now eat spinach, and just bought my first set of false eyelashes.

If what we're resenting is something we can change, then the path of least resistance is to acknowledge what is causing the resentment and then make the relevant changes to move away from resentment. For example, if I'm resenting that too much of the housework sits with me, I can either have a conversation with my family to reallocate the tasks of managing the home or look at other areas of responsibility that I currently hold that could be taken from me and given to Luke, our children, or even someone employed specifically for that purpose.

It feels like this should be an obvious lesson. Right? If you can't change something, why waste time resenting it? The logic is there. Unfortunately, we humans don't fully function in logic mode all the time. Our emotions have a way of welling up and taking over.

Probably the greatest evidence of this is that we often experience resentment over things from the past. There is literally nothing from the past that can be changed. No wishing, hoping, cursing, or crying can alter anything that has happened before this moment.

It may not always appear as resentment, but it can still pop up in other ways in relationships. How frustrating is it to not be able to change another person? Let's face it—we know what's best for them; why can't they just see it our way?!

If there's a sure-fire way to remove fulfilment and purpose from life, it's by resenting the inability to change people or our past or even the person we were in the past.

One theme that has come up repeatedly in interviews with experts on the radio show I do with my husband is the importance of asking good-quality questions. When do you most experience resentment? For example, is it when you're overworked and stressed? Or when you have too much time to think? What causes you the greatest feeling of resentment? Is the thing you're resenting really the thing you're resenting?

To face down resentment and kick it to the curb, we need an honest look at what it is that tends to stick as objects of resentment that are not able to be changed. At some point, we need to *give ourselves permission* to let go of those things that are unchangeable and that are actually robbing us of the joy and fulfilment that release us to be our best for both ourselves and those around us. As David Finch wrote in his article, *The Power of Permission*, 'More often than we realize, the only person telling us not to have fun is ourself.'[3]

For the things that can't be changed, that's where the work of this lesson really is.

Unchangeable resentments are predominantly in the past. Strangely, it's not big, awful things that happened to me. I had a stable upbringing, spared from many of the trials and challenges that are faced by all too many children. My resentments sit in what are, in reality, minor conflicts, embarrassing moments, or, almost ridiculously when I think of it, the passing harsh comments of strangers. I've fixated for all too long on being called fat, ugly, and looking like I'm constipated, even a sarcastic, 'Oh, you mean you can read' that came my way as I served in a newsagency as a teenager. I've made up witty comebacks, imagined myself powerful enough to hurt them more than

---

[3] Psychology Today (2013), David Finch, *The Power of Permission*, *Psychology Today*, viewed from, <https://www.psychologytoday.com/us/blog/the-journal-best-practices/201312/the-power-permission>.

they hurt me, and let their words seep into my soul and, at times, determine my self-worth. I can only imagine how much joy I've robbed myself of by being stuck in resentment of the unchangeable.

Sitting and writing it now almost gives me the power to look at it all as an outsider and see how valueless it all is. How easily these things have stolen joy and fulfilment from my life.

I feel there is real value in investigating further to see if we can flip the switch; don't you? Yes, it's critical to determine what can and can't be changed. To accept the unchangeable and to be courageous with the changeable. But, here's the switch. How much joy have I gained by having a heart that soft? If it has been hurt by so little, does it not also find joy in little? I look back and I realise that it absolutely does.

When I was at university, my friend Kate told me that she could find me by my laugh in the area of the university nicknamed the Great Court. In my first full-time job, another Kate told me that they knew things were stressful and busy when I stopped laughing as much. (NB If you don't have a friend called Kate, go and find one. They're amazing.)

I have always laughed easily. I cry with joy easily at the things that move me. Yes, I've lost too much time to unchangeable resentments, but I've also laughed longer at the joke, sat in the emotion longer of a moving performance, or lived longer in the happiness and celebration of a loved one. As I write this, it's a week since celebrating the wedding of a friend and the joy of that event has carried me this whole week. A week's worth of joy!

It's not the heart that needs to change—its softness serves to bring a deeper joy and fulfilment to life's experience. This lesson is about taking away something that steals joy and fulfilment unnecessarily.

Don't resent what you can't change. And then don't resent what you can change … just change it. Maybe the wisdom should just be to banish resentment altogether.

One thing I've done in my battle against resentment is to adopt a theme word for the year. A word for the year is just a word to help focus—a filter through which to make choices. My word this year is *simplify*.

I have to admit that I can get stuck on resentment about changeable things like finances, the mess of the walk-in robe, and the sheer quantity of laundry. So, this word, *simplify*, has helped me reframe that into a more solution-focused way of thinking. Believe me, resentment doesn't solve anything, it just prolongs a problem.

Simplify for me, this year, has meant looking for one thing each day that will remove an item from my mental load. I don't know about you, but my brain is always in overdrive. I think this is an adult condition—work, home, kids, friends, events, chores, self-care, and other—our brains have so much to think about each day, jumping from thing to thing. So, if I find myself obsessing about a problem such as the mess in the carport, *simplify* encourages me to fix one thing each day. I might not have the time or energy to clean the whole mess in the carport, but if I can clear a part of it, it helps enough to relieve some pressure. I'll be honest, quite a few of my days so far have been simplifying by forgetting that I'm supposed to be simplifying something. My strike rate is probably around sixty percent. Even so, it's definitely spared me some resentment by not letting me sit too long on problems that normally consume all-too-much brain space.

One example of overcoming a mental load with *simplify* occurred when I was feeling particularly overwhelmed with work. As well as recording the radio show, my role involves a significant amount of audio editing. I was feeling stressed about getting work done one week when I realised that my stress was caused by unreasonable timelines that I had created myself. There are deadlines for my work, but I had flouted those and determined that all my work should be done much quicker than it needed to be. It took me a while to realise that this was an issue of my own making because I thought I was buying time at the end of the week by completing the work sooner. Yet all I was actually doing was intensifying stress unnecessarily!

Once I became aware of what was going on, my simplifying task was to release the time pressure and, rather than trying to get three days' worth of work done in one day, I gave myself permission to do just that day's work. Yes, I'd have more work to do at the end of the week than my mind had originally planned, but the more even spread of tasks simplified the week overall.

So, let's look briefly at the other side of the coin. If we have to *not* resent the things we can't change, then it stands to reason that there could be fulfilment and purpose in taking hold of the things we can change, like our sheets and pyjamas. I hold it as a fundamental belief that fresh clean sheets and fresh clean pyjamas are the perfect end to any day. When it comes to looking at the flipside, it doesn't get much better.

I'm picturing it now. That moment, at the end of a day, when in the morning, the toast had burnt, then the traffic on the way to school made the boys late. Following that, the workday was far from smooth and flowing, filled with frustration and delays, and not accomplishing as much as was hoped for. Then, the critical ingredient for dinner wasn't there and what was meant to be spaghetti bolognese became some weird mincey/vegetabley dish that nobody finishes. But then … ah, then. In a fit of glorious wisdom, you change the sheets and pull out fresh sleepwear. In that glorious moment, it all washes away as you step into some fresh, clean pyjamas, and slide into those fresh clean sheets. It all changes with the letting go of the unchangeable and changing the simple thing we can.

Life Lesson: Don't resent what you can't change and don't keep resenting the things that you can change.

Takeaway: If you find yourself fixated on the resentment about something that you can't change, ask a better-quality question. Identify the true resentment and give yourself permission to let it go. When there's resentment where you do have control to change it, a focus word can help filter out resentment and create a pathway through to a solution. Also, clean sheets and fresh clean pyjamas are a beautiful way to end a day.

Questions:
- Is there any resentment that is playing on your mind?
- When you think of your current biggest challenge, is it a situation you can change, change part of, or not change at all?
- When you picture your life as filled with joy and delight, fulfilment and purpose, fun and meaning, what is one thing currently in your life that isn't in that picture?

Chapter 3:
ONE THING AT A TIME

It was only a few years ago that I first heard someone say that people can't multitask—they claimed we can only do one thing at a time. I bought it for a second and then threw it out, probably around the same time I grew two babies at once. Just to be clear, my youngest boys are twins.

Multitasking can become the norm in career, marriage, and parenthood. At work, it could be taking that phone call while you finish the email and, at the same time, shove that morsel of food in your mouth because this is the most time you'll have all day. In marriage, it's figuring out your calendar for the week while cooking dinner and simultaneously cleaning as you go. And parenthood, well, it's an endless stream of managing multiple needs simultaneously while keeping it all together.

As an example, here's an old Facebook post of mine from 2011, when my eldest was two and the twins were just over two months old.

Let's play a game. This morning I had one baby feeding and one baby screaming when my two-year-old appeared from down the hall with no pants on. What happened next?

The guesses that came from friends mostly involved the half-naked two-year-old creating a mess for me to clean up. But let me tell you what actually happened. The doorbell rang. That's what happened. A baby attached, a baby screaming, a two-year-old half-naked, and me answering the door to a shocked postman undoubtedly regretting his timing.

So don't tell me we're never really multitasking. We are flooded with tasks to do, and not doing them simultaneously just means we won't get them all done. I have to get the kids in the bath while dinner's on the stove or they won't get to bed on time. I have to send this email while

I finish dinner or the day won't start right tomorrow. I have to, I have to, I have to!

Unless … we actually don't.

What if it was okay if the kids didn't have a bath one night, or if bedtime was later, or if the email waited until after the dishes were done? What if the rules we've made aren't the rules at all, they're just expectations we've set? And what if we could change the expectations so that they weren't about tasks to be completed, but fulfilment and joy to be experienced?

Currently, I'm part of a writing group and we have all been encouraged to set aside the time to write without distractions. The problem is, we live in a world filled with distractions.

Whilst writing this section of the book, I'm sitting on the balcony of a hotel with a stunningly beautiful mountain and river view, and a boat full of people has just pulled into the dock below. It's a wonderful distraction to listen to their giggles and lively chats as they see the photos of themselves back at the shop. I'm one of those people that can't even watch a movie without distraction. Yes, I'm one of those frustrating people who watch a movie at home on the screen while playing a game on my phone. My attention is rarely focused completely on a task.

That kind of constant, unfocused attention is probably one of the biggest joy thieves in my life. It robs me of the ability to extract every little bit from the things that I do. Every bit of joy, or sadness, or hope, or purpose or accomplishment. It's just task, task, task, task, task—ticking off a list all day long until I return to the glorious bed, every so often in fresh pyjamas and with clean sheets.

This isn't just about doing one thing at a time, though; it's about handling each day better emotionally. I'm an easily frazzled monster. I can only imagine what I was like in that moment of baby feeding, baby screaming, a half-naked toddler, and the postman ringing the doorbell. My guess is frazzled.

Let me take you to where my brain is going right now. I may have unsuccessfully studied computer science, only learning to break life down into 'if, then, else' statements, but I do love maths. I really enjoy figuring stuff out. Maths, for the most part, is clear—there is right and there is wrong, and it is commonly agreed upon. If I have $1.50 and something is 50 cents, then I can buy three of them. The shop assistant agrees. If I take four and give only $1.50, the shop assistant disagrees, as do the manager and the police officer.

So, here's my maths on this topic. Remember the overall goal of this whole life lesson is greater joy and delight, fulfilment and purpose, fun and meaning—in other words, quality of life.

Focused attention equals days handled better. Days handled better equals a greater quality of life. Focused attention also equals less frazzle. Therefore, less frazzle equals a greater quality of life.

What does that all mean? Doing those things that help us to keep our mind straight, clear, and non-frazzled is to do things that are going to help bring a sense of joy, fulfilment, and probably, a greater sense of self or feeling better in your own skin.

With this in mind, the whole word-of-the-year experiment has led me to try something new recently and it's all been around focusing my attention at dinner time.

The default in my house is that dinner is my responsibility, but it's not always been a space that I've enjoyed. I actually like cooking, when I feel like I can just enjoy it, but with the family, pulling dinner together is often a rushed experience on the back of a day of work and running around with the kids while homework questions are fired at me or some version of 'Mum, my brother is doing something to me that I've done to him a thousand times before, but I want to get mad about it right now and make it your problem.' Enter my word of the year: *simplify*.

What I've done has been transformational. It's slowed me down, focused me 'in'. I do one thing—cook dinner—and I enjoy it a whole lot more and produce a better meal. So what's my secret? I put on an apron. That is literally the one thing I've changed, but in that one action, my whole being changes. Once that apron goes on, I'm cooking. That's my job. That's my focus.

Given that it's one of the last things I do at night, it's also made the end of my day a whole lot more enjoyable. An apron! Who'd have thunk it?

The kitchen has been a place that has highlighted how rough life is when doing multiple tasks. I can't tell you how many bowls, plates, serving dishes, cups, and glasses I've broken just because I'm trying to do too much too quickly just to get it done.

Luke and I are different in the way we approach tasks. I'm someone who just wants to get in, get the job done, and get out, whereas he wants to look at the job from a few different angles, figure out the best way and the best tools, work out the best strategy, and then methodically do the work. Ugh! My way gets the job done, sometimes shoddily, but it's done. Luke's way also gets the job done, sometimes late, sometimes exactly the way I would have done it if he'd just followed my advice in the first place, but it gets it done. But, my way often leads to me being, you guessed it—frazzled—because the whole time I'm just thinking about the moment I can say, 'That'll do', and move on to the next task.

I'd like to say that Luke's way, being more focused, always results in the best outcome. But let me tell you one story. We had a car with automatic windows. We'd been visiting family who lived a few hours away and, as evening set in, we put the boys in the back of the car, rolled down the windows to wave goodbye, and clunk … the passenger side window wouldn't go back up. It was a bit on the chilly side already, the drive ahead of us was over four hours long and mostly highway driving at 100 km/h, so you can imagine how cold it was going to get. We're inventive, so we grabbed a shirt to cover the window and made do.

The next day, Luke set about fixing the window so it would go up. He did his usual method—went about researching, figured out the best and most cost-effective source of parts, watched YouTube videos to help him along, and then step by step fixed the window. It was fantastic. In the end, the passenger side window was all fixed. Yay! Along the way, though, Luke snapped the handle off the door and broke the driver's side window. At this point, you'd think, *That's okay, if he just does his process again, he can fix those things, and all will be well.*

Two and a half years later, Luke finally got around to fixing the driver's side window. He followed his process and, after getting what he needed, it was a 45-minute job. He was so proud of himself. He called me out to show me what he'd done. And, at the end of his demonstration, four hours and two and a half years after the initial window got stuck, none of the windows worked and the driver's side window was stuck down.

In the end, if the journey is towards greater fulfilment and joy, then diminishing the frazzle by focusing on one thing at a time will usually work as a step in the right direction. As we learn from Luke, it doesn't always work out, but the goal is better, not perfect. As a bonus life lesson, maybe don't get Luke to fix things.

PS We ended up getting a new (second-hand) car with working windows. One day, I'll tell you the story of how it rolled itself into a church with no people around.

Life Lesson: Slow down and do one thing at a time where you can.

Takeaway: Trying to be efficient by multitasking might get the job done, but it may also rob joy, delight, fulfilment, purpose, fun and meaning from each of the individual tasks. Slowing down might just help us see that some of the best of life is in the doing, not just in the completing of tasks.

Questions:

- Are you multitasking parts of your life unnecessarily?
- What is one regular, unavoidable job/task/chore in your life you would like to enjoy more?
- Where are you successfully focusing on one thing at a time in your life?

Chapter 4:
JUMPING IN PUDDLES

I'm starting to think that I don't like movies. If I go to the cinema, then it's okay. Movies at home are another thing. I just don't have an interest in committing that amount of time to the story. So, I sit with a movie on, playing a game on my phone, scrolling social media, planning radio shows, searching real estate, sorting my finances, organising the calendar, or any number of other things. When it comes to a movie at home, I'm happy to walk away with just the gist of it.

So, maybe movies aren't my thing. Maybe jumping in puddles is my thing.

This life lesson is one I remember learning clearly. The twins were around two years old, and our eldest was about four. There'd been quite a bit of rain so there'd been an unusually lengthy stint of indoor time with the children. We hadn't been to the park or the beach or the pool. On this one day, I headed out to check the mailbox and the boys came bouncing out with me. They went straight for the gutter and jumped.

I ran the boys all back inside, not to stop them, but to get some rain boots on them so we could really commit to the task. And we jumped and kicked and splashed and jumped and jumped and jumped. We giggled and played. It was one of those moments where we were really present together and just enjoying the moment.

If I think back to the time in my life when the joy and fulfilment and the feeling of being right in my skin was there, then it was a time when there was more of this.

*

I remember a time back at university. I was living in a house off campus and a friend came around and we had a tendency for silliness together. It was how we cheered each other up, had fun and created memories and stories.

I can't remember why we did this, but we put on formal dresses, grabbed some sports gear, and stood on the side of the road, posing for passing cars. Some honked their horns, although most drove by without us seeing a reaction, yet we laughed and played and created a life story.

I've sat in Hungry Jacks in a bridesmaid dress, I've danced in the kitchen, and made up rap songs. I've made a musical with dolls, acted out episodes of TV shows, and changed the rules of almost every game I've ever played. And I've jumped in puddles.

As time goes on, it's this stuff that falls away bit by bit. I don't know if it's our perception of how adults behave, or if it's self-consciousness that prevents us from doing things we'll be judged for. Or is it lethargy or the busyness of life that gets in the way? Whatever it is, it's time to reclaim the silliness.

Children help keep this side of ourselves alive for a while. But then they start to grow up and hit a point where they can be embarrassed by our very existence, let alone our public displays of silliness.

It shouldn't stop us, though. It's time for us to fight back. Reclaim the silliness. Let go of the self-consciousness and claim the joy of letting the sillies out.

I was driving home after school drop-off the other day, and the traffic light turned red as I got to it. Ahead of me, some people were crossing the road. There was an older gentleman, a young man, and an older woman wearing headphones. It looked like the young man and the woman knew each other, but the young man kept walking ahead of her, then waiting for her to catch up, then walking ahead, then stopping to wait for her to catch up. I didn't understand why he was walking ahead of her until I watched her cross the road. This woman is a role model. She crossed the road normally for about three-quarters of the crossing, then my best guess is that the beat kicked in, and let me tell you, she had moves! She was dancing her way towards wherever they were going, and she was amazing. I looked over to see the young man waiting impatiently for her to catch up. I figured then that they were mother and son. If I could imagine what they were thinking, my best guess is that his head was screaming, *MUUUUUM!!!* and her head was filled with singing and *woohooos!* Whatever they were actually thinking, I can tell you who had the better time out on their walk that day.

I did Zumba with a friend for a while, and it was so good. It gave me exercise every week, time with my friend and, inevitably, the sillies always came out one way or another. The instructor was a beautiful friend of mind whose philosophy for Zumba is that there are no wrong moves, only awesome solos. So, the pressure is off. If you can't follow the moves, just keep moving, do your own thing, and bust out an awesome solo! For me, I interpreted that as 'just shake something', which is easy for me, because I just have to do a small move and things keep shaking for a while. It was safe, it was fun, and on more than one occasion, I literally ended up on the floor laughing.

And then life got in the way.

I think my favourite expression of the sillies is in a fun exchange with friends. Giving a joke gift, being in on a surprise, or a fun prank. I love those things where the act itself has no value except in the surprise, delight, and joy it brings to those on the receiving end.

I loved being in on a prank an old co-worker played on Luke one time, especially since I didn't have to do any of the work. Back then, he was the content director of a radio station in Melbourne, and the night's announcer, an amazing young woman named Jesse, decided she was going to prank Luke for Christmas. After Luke left the office and before he arrived the next morning, her mission was to wrap every single thing in his office. Every. Single. Thing. It was impressive. She brought a team of friends and family in to help, and they worked tirelessly until midnight. There was even a dead fly that was wrapped. My job was to get up the stairs of the office before Luke to film him as he walked in. After all her efforts, she wasn't even going to be there to watch his reaction! What they'd done was a marvel. Her selfless silliness brought so much joy and I can't even count the number of times the story has been told.

There's so much advice out there these days about minimising stress and anxiety in our lives. This lesson is just about increasing the good. The joy stuff. Taking the moments when that flicker of silliness comes into your mind and, rather than talking yourself out of it, seize the moment and do the silly thing! It's not a waste of time, it's a quality use of time to do something that adds joy to you and those around you. Sure, the people around you might look at you like you're weird, but they're just not ready to seize the silliness yet.

Luke's the king of seizing that moment that comes into his mind. There was a time when we'd been living in a house for a while and the garage had become a messy and disorganised storage room. So rather than do the overwhelming job of tidying all of it in one go, we decided to break it down into 20-minute chunks and tackle it a bit at a time.

On our first night, we headed into the garage, picked the area where we'd start, and got into it. Armed with gloves, shoes, and garbage bags, we set the clock for twenty minutes. I headed for a corner and started sorting. Luke found a jacket and then modelled it, telling me tales of how he would enjoy it for the few days of winter next season. Five minutes. Then, he found cricket pads and told himself tales of how good they still were. Six minutes. I asked him to move two weights. He made a joke about how he would do it if I did ten reps of lifting them, laughed heartily, and then moved them. Five minutes. He then picked up three things. Four minutes.

BBBBBBZZZZZZZZZZZZZ!!!! Time's up.

It was inconvenient timing. The garage needed to be tidied, but in this case, it made the time pass quicker and we (read: me … ALL ME! … though he'll claim the royal 'we') made a pretty big dent in the work that night.

It would be great to master this manner of working—to find fun in the midst of the task—on the way to greater joy and fulfilment. The truth is that my current state is easily absorbed into stress and the tasks. As I try to find my way back to the place where I feel like 'me' again, even though I laugh a lot, there's a light-heartedness that has gone AWOL for a while now, lost in the midst of business, family, and life.

For a time, I think taking life a bit more seriously has carried me through to do what had to be done, but now I can let Serious Susie go and return to being a person who would have an unpredictable reaction if pranked. Seriously, if someone had tried to significantly prank me in the last few years, I don't know if I would have laughed, cried, or yelled. It would have depended on the day.

Life Lesson: Sometimes the best thing to do is jump in puddles.

Takeaway: Embrace the silliness. Jump in the puddles, sing at the top of your lungs, dance in the kitchen. Life is too short to not take the opportunity to make some deliberate fun and to fully immerse yourself in it.

Questions:
- When was the last time you did something purely for fun?
- Picture a moment in your life when you remember feeling joy and delight to your very core. What were you doing? Who were you with? What made the moment so memorable?
- What is one thing you enjoy doing for the fun of it?

Chapter 5:
JUST TRY

The challenge hits regularly. I pull up to the house. The car boot is opened. Can I get into the kitchen with all of these shopping bags in one trip? I might not make it every time, but I'll never stop trying. Some weeks, this is the only strength training I get.

You never know what you're capable of until you try. Our capacity, individually, is determined by a lot of different factors. Some people set personal limits based on upbringing, education, or finances. Others seem to determine their capacity based on the sun, the moon, and the stars. The difference between them is a willingness to try—to step out of the norm, away from the predictable, and into that zone where comfort is so far in the rear vision mirror it's just a dot.

I get the theory; I often fail at the practice. What can I say? I'm a big fan of the comfort zone. That's why it's called the comfort zone. I'm comfortable there.

Life often has different plans for us, though, and a willingness to follow the cues can lead us toward a life beyond our expectations.

In my life, I feel like there's a pattern of me saying, 'I'll never (add thing I've decided I'll never do here)' only to find myself constantly in the position where that thing that I've decided I'll never do becomes the next good choice in my life. It's frustrating and it always shows up how little I know myself. Before you ask, yes, I have tried saying, 'I'll never be ridiculously wealthy' and 'I'll never win an Oscar' in an effort to force them into being, but those things have so far eluded me.

Just before my final year at university, I went on a mission trip to India for a few weeks.

It was an incredible experience to share with the rest of the team and one that I'll treasure my whole life. At Hyderabad, a small stop on our long trip, we visited a ministry called NATIVE, and one of their staff offered phrasebooks for their local language. A few of our team took them up on the offer, but I remember scoffing, saying, 'Why? I'll never be back here.' Before the year was through, I decided to go back to India and work in that ministry for a year. That's what happens when I say, 'Never.'

The year in India was incredible and showed me more of my capacity. My days were filled with administration work, coordinating events, teaching English, and even working at a printing press for a while. I lived among the locals and learnt a little of the language and have lived life ever since with a longing to return.

After India, I spent a few years working for World Vision, an international aid organisation. I learnt so much there and was grateful to have an incredible boss who developed me up through the ranks. Throughout that time, I came into contact with the local radio station, which I loved, and had little bits to do with here and there. I was asked if I'd ever considered going into radio, and my response was, 'No, I'd never be brave enough.' I had my first stint on air in radio nearly two decades ago. That's what happens when I say, 'Never.'

Two days before I was to be a bridesmaid at my friend's wedding, she told me about this guy and said she thought we'd be great together. She described him as a bit shorter than me, with a stocky build, and loud—what Luke now describes as short, fat, and feral. I walked down the aisle at her beautiful wedding, turned around, saw this guy standing there who was staring at me, and thought to myself, *Quit staring, you freak*, followed by, *Knowing my luck I'll end up married to that guy*. (Note: I'm not proud of these thoughts, but I distinctly remember them as direct quotes from my brain.) Needless to say, the attraction wasn't instant. As I sit here, I've been married to that short, fat, feral man since 2003. Sure, I didn't specifically say, 'Never,' but it was certainly implied in my sarcasm.

You'd think I'd learn to keep myself open by never saying that I'd never do something, but I'm yet to learn the lesson definitively. I have since found myself doing things I never thought I'd do all too many times. And each time, I'm grateful.

The reality is, in saying I'd never do something, I'm essentially saying that I don't see it for myself. I'm so glad that my potential and capacity have been so much further beyond my own expectations. I'm also grateful to have said yes to all of those 'nevers' along the way, because they've shaped so much in my life that I love.

There are people in my world who have had a clear plan for their lives. They've known all along what they were working towards. They've worked hard with clear focus, and bit by bit, it's been amazing to watch them smash goal after goal towards each dream they've held.

Unfortunately, I am not one of those people. A clear vision isn't something that I've held for my life. I've taken opportunities, learnt along the way, and bit by bit, been surprised by the life that has unfolded before me. As a teenager, I had a clear vision. I was going to become an accountant, marry a taller and older man, and live my life swimming in money surrounded by numbers.

Instead, I've been a missionary, worked for a charity, been a temp, worked in a church, been a personal assistant, stayed at home as a mum, and have spent years now working in radio both on and off the air. I married a man who is both shorter and younger and have had fluctuating financial circumstances, especially through the time of starting up our business.

Swimming in money has not been the experience.

As for children—when I was young, I couldn't picture myself as a mum. I was never natural with children and just didn't see myself as someone who would enjoy being a parent. I married at twenty-eight, and we wanted kids, then didn't want kids, then wanted kids, then didn't want kids. Eventually, it became the single focus for us to have children. After making that decision, it was another four and a half years before we fell pregnant, and then met our firstborn Tyson through in-vitro fertilisation. After Tyson, we had one remaining embryo, which we transferred when we felt ready, but it was unsuccessful. It didn't take long to start to love the idea of life being just the three of us. The next month, we fell pregnant naturally with twins. Each child has added richness to my life. They are so different from each other and I'm incredibly grateful for all three of them.

I remember a friend of ours saying that every baby felt wrong in his arms until he had his own and that was absolutely my experience. I still wouldn't describe myself as a natural parent and my decisions along the way have often been far from logical, but we've muddled our way through, and so far, have been rewarded with three healthy, growing, thriving young men, each with their own gifts, personality, and passions.

For me, children are a separate category from the other things in my world where I've proven more capable through trying. Yes, they have been amazing capacity-builders, but I know we could just as easily have not been able to have children. You can't earn the right to children; it's not a case of the deserving that get them and the undeserving don't. We don't have full control of the outcome of wanting children. So, for me, they are a remarkable gift, and I am grateful for each one.

Finding out what we're capable of is about homing in on the things within our control and not settling in spaces where we feel dissatisfied. I have a beautiful friend who was complaining about how the world kept telling her she should want more in her life, and she posed the question, 'What's so wrong with the simple life? I love the life we've built.' For me, that's the dream. There's no dissatisfaction there. She's comfortable in her skin, fulfilled, happy, and purpose-filled. That is the dream. This book, and this desire to strive to find what I'm capable of, is an attempt to treat the dissatisfaction, the feeling of not quite being myself, and that gap in fulfilment.

Each week we do a 'Would You Rather' segment and this question was sent to us by a listener named Steven. 'Would you rather short legs and long arms, or short arms and long legs?' I'll give you a minute to figure out your answer.

We have so much fun with these questions. Luke always gets mad when people try to sit on the fence, and every week, you can guarantee someone will try to find the loophole. This question stood out to me, though.

I kept wondering what each person pictured. How long were the arms and how short were the legs? Was it orangutan vs. T-rex, or was it just legs or arms that were short, but the human tall? Or were the legs or arms long, but the human short?

While the 'Would You Rather' segment is quirky and gives our imaginations a fun workout, the deeper questions can push us out of our comfort zone. When the question is, 'You never know what you're capable of until you try', do you picture yourself climbing Mount Everest, winning a Grammy, or saving the world from climate change? Or do you picture yourself finishing that novel, losing that weight, or restoring that relationship?

The question is relative to each of us, and I guess, in some way, our answers might identify how far we feel from being fulfilled or comfortable in our own skin.

Right now, I'm wondering if we, as a family, are capable of keeping the house clean for more than three days. Will I ever fold a fitted sheet without it looking just like it did in the laundry basket before I folded it? Will I get to a point where I feel more comfortable in my body? Will I finish this book? Will I learn the guitar?

As a wise man once said, 'Do or do not. There is no try.' Okay, it was Yoda. Still, I completely disagree. All along the way to the 'do' or 'do not' is us trying, getting braver, stepping out of our comfort zones and often uncertain of whether the ultimate outcome of our trying will result in success or failure. This is the moment I realise I wouldn't have been a Jedi. Does that mean I'd be a bad guy? I haven't watched enough of the movies to know.

Still, stepping out to try something new or to do something in a new way is a far more appealing prospect where the known outcome, regardless of success or failure, is a sense of fulfilment and joy in having tried.

Life Lesson: You never know what you're capable of until you try.

Takeaway: Be open to opportunities and willing to develop capacity through trying, even if the end result isn't what you wanted.

Questions:
- When was the last time you were out of your comfort zone?
- Have you ever found yourself doing something that you'd previously said you'd never do? What was the outcome?
- What is one thing you have never done but have always wanted to do?

Chapter 6:
PEOPLE ARE DIFFERENT

I recently attended a wedding with my husband, Luke. It was on a Saturday, and we had to get up early to take our eldest off to the skateboard park after a late Friday night. It was also the day before a family event that we do every year, which involves a special breakfast with all the trimmings and sharing around the table what we love about each other.

Given how busy the week had been, I wasn't quite prepared for the Sunday breakfast when Saturday rolled around. I had all the decorations sorted, but there was still some food that needed to be bought before we left for the wedding.

So, I got up early, did the skatepark with our eldest, got home around 8.45, and then sat with Luke to work out how we were going to do what needed to be done before the wedding. I'd put the wedding location into the Maps app on my phone the night before. According to it, we needed to leave at 1.30 pm to give ourselves time to get there and be settled before the wedding started.

As we sat at the dining table, coffee in hand and the smell of toast in the air from the boys' breakfasts, we set our plan.

Luke needed to get a haircut and a pair of shoes, so since he'd be out anyway, he'd get the groceries for the Sunday breakfast as well. He left around 9.30 am.

Just before midday rolled around, I decided to start getting myself ready for the wedding.

I had a shower. Luke wasn't home yet. I had a small lunch. Luke wasn't home yet. I put on my make-up. Luke wasn't home yet. I blow-dried my hair. Luke still wasn't home. I got dressed for the wedding. Still no Luke.

When I was all done, I sat at that same dining table where we'd planned out the day and watched the time roll by. I tried to call him. No answer. I eventually got through on the phone at 12:58 pm, thirty-two minutes before we had to leave, and he was standing in the supermarket at a shop about fifteen minutes away. At 1.30 pm, I got a text message saying, *I am just about to arrive. Can you send the boys out?* The boys always help Luke bring the groceries in because he's not as brave as me at the game of 'Can I get all these bags inside in one trip?'

He walks through the door, now after the time we had to leave, goes into our bedroom, and emerges eight minutes later completely ready to go.

I did my very best to control my frustration as we headed to the car. He opened the door for me, and we finally left for the wedding. At this point, I opened up my Maps app to get the route so I could navigate for him, only to realise that I had calculated our travel time to the wedding based on our going by bicycle. So, yep ... turns out we had plenty of time to get there.

The next morning, it's special breakfast time and I have the plan in my head. I need to decorate the table, cook the bacon, eggs, pancakes, plain croissants, and ham and cheese croissants, toast the bagels, get the juice and water on the table, and make the teas and coffees. The one thing Luke hadn't been able to get the day before was bacon. I mean seriously, what supermarket sells out of bacon?! So, Luke was put in charge of buying the bacon from a shop that is a 2-minute drive away, and we'd share whatever tasks were left when he got home.

So, Luke leaves to buy the bacon. I make the pancake batter, set and decorate the table, cook the pancakes, get the juice and water on the table, bake the plain croissants and the ham and cheese croissants, cook the eggs, and at this point, start thinking, *Where is Luke*? I was literally on the last job—making the hot drinks—when Luke walked through the door, bacon in hand and with two coffees from my favourite coffee shop, which had taken him well out of his way and added the extra time to his shopping trip. He jumped straight to work, cooking the bacon on the barbecue, and everything was on the table at the same time.

We were at the wedding early and had a wonderful time, and the family breakfast was lovely to be a part of. It could have all been dampened by my expectation that Luke work the way I work and by me spending a disproportionate amount of time frustrated by his poor time management and questionable decision-making.

I should clarify. The reason it took Luke so long to get a haircut, buy shoes, and do the grocery shopping on that specific Saturday was that, at each point along the way, he kept adding another thing. He went to get a modem, went to buy pants, and tried to sort out another tech issue that included him being on a waiting list where they called him back when they were ready.

We are different. We make vastly different decisions. We attack problems differently.

We interpret experiences differently. We parent differently. We partner differently.

For all too long, this has brought frustration, anxiety, stress, anger, hurt, and befuddlement. All of that is something that is within my power to change with a simple attitude adjustment.

I can, instead, choose to have these differences bring me joy, learning opportunities, humility, gratitude, laughter, and connection.

People are different and that should be celebrated.

*

The world is a funny place. On the one hand, we spend our whole childhood going through school, where we have to behave a certain way, look a certain way, treat others a certain way, and learn a certain way. Belonging is in being the same as others and living the way others say it is done.

Then, as an adult, you start to get told that if you want to make a difference, you have to stand out from the crowd, be different, think differently, have a different perspective, and bring different skills. The people we often admire stepped out from the norm and did things despite everyone around them saying it couldn't be done.

It's a tough switch to flick. As adults, we struggle with people seeing things differently from us. If you want an example, tune into parliament sometime or participate in a social media debate. What is implied in our behaviour is that if you think differently from me, then you are thinking the wrong thing and, quite frankly, that makes you someone of less value, of less worth, and it's okay to disrespect you.

Ridiculous, right?

We aren't designed to think the same as each other, behave the same as each other, or have the same perspectives as each other. Herein lies the choice. Will we be frustrated, disappointed, and live with expectations of others that are unrealistic? Or will we be teachable, respectful, and understanding?

I can't see my way back to a joyfully fulfilled, comfortable-in-her-own-skin me by choosing Option A.

To be honest, there's some self-protection in this one as well. I've been hideously empathic and self-conscious my whole life. Basically, I've lived presuming, in my mind, how others have judged me and have used it as a tool to beat myself throughout adulthood. I empathically pick up a feeling, and then, I impose judgments to that on myself.

If the lesson is to delight in the differences of others, then maybe I can let go of the expectation that others delight in the difference of me. If I feel myself having an empathic response of judgment from others, I can simply appreciate it as a way that someone perceives, experiences, and interprets differently from me, and then, let it go.

They say that there's a freedom that comes in your 40s and I think it's starting to really kick in now. It could even be a catalyst to significantly reducing my brain's determination to destroy me emotionally.

There's a freedom that Luke has had in this space that I've admired for a long time. He's impacted significantly less by the opinion of others. In fact, he has chosen carefully whose opinion in his life he'll give credit to and whose doesn't matter. He associates widely with people and thrives in taking on different perspectives on issues. He loves battling the opposite side of a debate to what he believes because it helps him learn something of another side of the argument. He withholds judgment until he knows more facts from both sides, and he doesn't make decisions about people based on the opinion of others. Some of these skills I've been grateful to learn as I've walked through life beside him.

Coming to understand the concept of grace has been an incredible part of getting me on the way to conquering this life lesson. I held on to the black-and-white of life for a long time, but a few years ago, I realised that life isn't black and white. There's a whole spectrum of colour out there and, for the most part, everyone is doing the best they can with what they know and with what they have. Few people are deliberately the bad guy, and so don't see themselves that way in most scenarios. So, in any situation, there's a good chance that there's a whole lot of backstory or information we don't know. All this is is to say we can just enjoy the fact that people are different to us without having to stamp right, wrong, or otherwise on them or ourselves. There is an opportunity to keep learning instead of just staying in a monochromatic life.

Life Lesson: Enjoy the fact that people are different.

Takeaway: There is joy, delight, fulfilment and purpose, fun and meaning in appreciating people's differences and releasing ourselves from any expectation that people should think, act, and feel the way that we do. It is our differences that make life interesting.

Questions:

- Think of the key people of influence in your world. What are some of the key differences between you and how does that add value to your relationship?
- What is something different about you that makes you add value to your work/family/ community?
- Is there any hurt or resentment you are carrying because of your expectations of another person?

Chapter 7:

YOU CAN TEACH AN OLD DOG NEW TRICKS

We were living in a house in a complex on the Gold Coast that had a large pool. The twins had been doing swimming lessons and Tyson, our eldest, was getting braver and bolder in the pool all the time.

This one day, he started doing somersaults into the pool. He'd somersault in, get out, go back to the deep end, and somersault in again. He was having so much fun. I can't remember who he'd learnt from, but seeing him master the skill was great to watch. So good, in fact, that it made me want to do some. The only problem was, I had never learnt to somersault into the pool. I could somersault forwards and backwards if I was in the pool, but I never learned to flip forwards or backwards into the pool from the deck like my sister. Timidity ruled me in this space.

I told Tyson how much fun it looked and this little child of mine looked back at me and said, 'Do you want me to teach you?' He would have been four years old at the time. The protective part of my brain kicked into gear and screamed, 'No!' Then, the other part of my brain kicked in, you know, that Mummy brain, and she started yelling at the first part of the brain, saying, 'No, you have to do this!' Mummy brain won and I jumped out of the pool to become the first student at Tyson's somersault-into-the-pool school.

He explained to me that I had to crouch right down and, when I was ready, just do a somersault into the pool. As regret flooded my body, I realised that being a student meant actually having to follow through and do a somersault into the pool. I racked my brain to come up with a decent excuse for a four-year-old: 'Fireman Sam said mummies shouldn't do this', 'I can't crouch down anymore because there are very bad consequences for the pool deck', 'I'll get to it in lesson two next week' … hoping he'd forget. None of them made it from my genius brain to my mouth, though. I decided to go with 'toughen up, princess,' and proceeded to get down low and go, go, go, performing my first somersault into the pool. In my head, it scored an 8.9.

It was so much fun! I started doing exactly what Tyson had been doing. Both of us somersaulting in, getting out, walking around, and doing it over and over again.

It's moments like these that show up how much we can miss out on by listening to the wrong part of the brain. For me, this was such a special experience that I easily could have sabotaged by disengaging when my brain first said no. I would have missed out on all the fun and the closeness I felt with my son, at the time.

I mentioned earlier in the book what a bad student I was, as highlighted by my inability to log into a computer when I was doing computer science at university. I've had to get my head around the fact that I've been making a blanket statement about myself based on an experience from nearly three decades ago. Yikes!

One of the key phrases going around now is 'limiting beliefs'. 'I'm a bad student' is a limiting belief and it's time to chuck it out the window and bring in a new idea.

Cognitive behaviour therapy (or CBT) is, in simple terms, a process of taking a thought process that isn't working for you and replacing it with a new one.[4] For example, instead of saying, 'I'm a bad student,' it could be replaced with, 'I like to learn in creative ways.'

With the rate at which the world around us is changing and technology is improving, the best mindset to take into this next life stage—the fulfilled, joyful, feeling good in myself one—is to be a learner. I need to be an old dog pretending to be a young dog and be open to learning new tricks. Kind of like how our little dog pretends to be a big dog and is open to being chased or chasing others in the park.

There's so much I've always wanted to learn—guitar, a different language, basic car mechanics, sewing, and other. Gymnastics may have passed me by, but there is so much out there. I'd love to get a boat license, and maybe even, at some point, a further qualification in … I don't know what yet. I also wouldn't mind learning more about the backstories of the people in my world with whom I spend so much time.

The good news is that this is an easy lesson to conquer. Some of the other life lessons are easy to say, they make sense to explain, but in practice, it's a process. This one is measurable. Did I learn something new today? Well, yes.

---

[4] BioPsychoSocial Medicine – BMC (2021), Nakao, M., Shirotsuki, K., and Sugaya, N., *Cognitive-behavioral therapy for management of mental health and stress-related disorders: Recent advances in techniques and technologies,* viewed from, <https://bpsmedicine.biomedcentral.com/articles/10.1186/s13030-021-00219-w>.

I learnt that my son has access to be able to make in-app purchases and he needs to be more closely monitored.

Everyone in my home is a learner. The boys are all at various stages of their formal education and are enjoying learning new things every day at school. Luke has a naturally curious mind and is always looking for opportunities to learn something new. The great thing about having a home full of learners is that, like being around a smoker, you become a passive learner.

Around the dinner table, it's common for any one or all of the boys, including Luke, to share something that they learnt that day. I've learnt all too much about Googlebots and meta data from Luke.

The gap, for me, is taking control of what I'm learning. The goal is to no longer be a passive learner, but to be an active learner. What are the things I could learn about that would bring joy? What are things that will add value to my life and the lives of those I serve? What can I learn that will fill some gaps in my understanding of the world around me?

Along the way, we realise that it's not just that there's so much to learn, but that we may have picked up a few things that we need to unlearn. We need to unlearn rules that we've based our life on that actually aren't rules at all, they're just limiters. We need to unlearn lies about people in our life that we've believed and held against them. We need to unlearn habits that no longer serve us and steal richness from our experience of the everyday.

Back in the land before the pandemic, when the world was open and we freely went about without sanitising our hands at every stop and checking in to every building we walked near, Luke and I had a date night at the movies.

From memory, we splurged and went Gold Class, with the extra-comfortable, reclining chairs and food and drink delivered mid-movie. It's always a bit of a treat and we had a great time. That is, until the drive home.

The movie we watched was one of those whodunnits. On the way home, we were both saying how much we loved the movie and then Luke said something like, 'When did you figure it out?' Well, I did what any decent human being would do at this point and simply answered the question. And that's the end of the story.

Unfortunately, that's not what I did. I absolutely lost my cool. I got so angry, so quickly. I started going on about how I hate feeling like I'm constantly being tested and if you want to tell me when you figured it out, just tell me when you figured it out, don't ask me first so you can come in afterwards and tell me how you beat me to figuring it all out. I was absolutely off the chain ranting. We were now close to home and the conversation had erupted to the point where Luke pulled the car over so that we had a chance to cool down before we got back to our kids and babysitter. Sounds reasonable, right?

Wrong! I jumped on the opportunity to really double down, and I got out of the car, slammed the door, and walked all the way home.

Eventually, when we came back into the same space and the figurative smoke emanating from my body had eased, we sat down and started to break apart what had just happened.

What we discovered was that, after seventeen years of marriage, we had some things we needed to unlearn about how we were communicating and some things we needed to learn if we wanted to avoid another outbreak of 'World War Susan' on an unsuspecting, innocent question.

By the way, the question wasn't intended to entrap me. Luke asked the question because he actually hadn't figured it out beforehand at all.

It turns out, I'd been holding onto some things, such as hating being asked pop quiz questions in a conversation. Seriously, if you want to say something, just say it; don't throw metaphorical logs in front of people just so you can feel good about yourself when they trip over them. Maybe I'm still holding onto some things here. To be honest, I'm quite confident that, along the way, I've been the log-thrower at times in my life and, knowing how it makes me feel, I don't want to make others feel that way.

Being an old dog doesn't disqualify us from learning new things, whether in skill, knowledge, or relationships. You can be in the same job for thirty years and still learn something new to do things better, not because the role has changed, but because everything around us has changed and we need to change with it. We've learnt through the pandemic that adaptability is a quality life skill and adapting is just a form of learning something new and changing with it.

It was Maya Angelou who said, 'I did then what I knew how to do. Now that I know better, I do better.'[5] We are the winners when we are willing to be learners.

Life Lesson: You can teach an old dog new tricks.

---

[5] Oprah's LifeClass (2011), *The Powerful Lesson Maya Angelou Taught Oprah*, viewed from, <https://www.oprah.com/oprahs-lifeclass/the-powerful-lesson-maya-angelou-taught-oprah-video>.

Takeaway: We can shrug off the 'old dog' label, treat ourselves like a scruffy little puppy, and learn a little something every day. There's a joy to be experienced, fulfilment to be gained, and a greater depth of understanding that enables us to do better as a result. Learning takes place not just in developing skills, but in developing and strengthening our relationships, and it's designed to bring us closer to joy and delight, fulfilment and purpose, fun and meaning.

Questions:

- What is a skill that you would like to learn?
- When was the last time you learnt something new and how has it added value to your life?
- Is there a key relationship in your world where you would both benefit from learning a new way to relate to each other?

Chapter 8:
WHAT'S YOUR OPINION?

I'd call myself a people-pleaser. All too many decisions in my life have been made based on what I think *someone else* thinks is the best decision. It's made me unsure of my own mind, and it's made me lose confidence in my own instincts. So, the idea of understanding that opinions have far less value than we think is a critical life lesson for me.

Others don't think about you nearly as much as you think, so there's very little value in trying to please them. Also, our opinion of others has no bearing on their worth or decision-making, so there's no point in over-investing in a bad opinion of another person. All it does is cause unnecessary stress over something that literally has no good outcome or benefit. Opinions never determine a person's worthiness, potential, and value.

You can spend your life trying to please the people in your world whose opinion you've decided is the most important, but if it takes something you do to make them feel good, then maybe they need to start their own journey towards greater joy, peace, fulfilment, and feeling good in their own skin.

Those who are pleased by what you do will be pleased by anything you do, because chances are they love you and don't have nearly the expectations on you that you think. And those who aren't pleased, likely won't be pleased regardless of what you do, so what do you have to lose?

As for the other side, someone who's hurt you or who, for whatever reason, you've developed a dislike or hatred for, can publicly fail and be hit with as much bad stuff as you can imagine for them. But let me tell you that if you're actually wishing that for them, they're no longer the only bad guy in the situation. No ill-wish, no matter how much they've hurt you, will change the value of the person you're investing so much mental and emotional energy in. It just doesn't.

If it did, then the person who you've hurt, deliberately or otherwise, or who for whatever reason has determined you as their object of hatred, can determine your value. And I just say a big NO to that.

People-pleasing and people-hating are just destructive patterns to be in.

I say this all very boldly for someone who's lost years of her life to both of them. I've been so good at both of them that they eventually crossed over.

On more than one occasion, I've imagined future arguments with people who I was trying to people-please. Then, when the future me didn't please them, I mentally walked my way through the hurt of it all and fought it out in my head. It's a sad, sad mastery of a destructive skill.

As with all things, having the realisation of the senseless-ness of it all can easily lead to another mental battle of guilt and shame for the time that's been lost. Instead, the more effective choice is to find a better thought to swap in.

That doesn't mean we can't learn anything from people-pleasing. There might be things we've achieved that we wouldn't have if we hadn't been motivated to please others. There are things that we've gained through the process that can serve us in the future. Hopefully, as we look back on it all, we can start to recognise the things that actually brought us joy that we mightn't have tried otherwise.

If we can take an honest look at the people we've lost the most time over and the trigger that started it all, maybe we can learn things about what not to do. What to avoid is just as valuable in life as what to do. Then, when we feel brave, we can use our minds to help us move on. In the same way we argued with people in our head, we can thank them for what they taught us and leave them where they belong—in our unchangeable past.

When we had a special breakfast as a family recently, we went around the table saying what we loved about each other. One of the things Luke spoke to me about was how my brain works overtime and how tiring that must be for me to be thinking about so much all the time.

As I pool together the last chapter with this one, I can't help thinking how much better use it would be to put my mind towards learning. If I could take the effort my brain uses on mental arguments and people-pleasing and, instead, applied that level of effort to learning, then I should pretty much be at professor level in every possible field by this time next year. I mean, I might even remember everyone's birthday.

Which begs the question, if we're no longer doing the people-pleasing or harbouring negativity towards people, what do we do with all that free time and free mental space? Do we just fall straight to sleep at night?

Maybe we could use it for things like making sure the next roll of toilet paper is always close by. If I'd learnt this lesson earlier, I would have used the free mental space to make a better decision about whether or not to try the kidney dish that Luke cooked one night. I chose to eat it.

I shouldn't have. A freer mind would have seen that one coming.

I think back on the first years of marriage with Luke. One issue that came up time and time again was the fact that Luke had really clear passions and I just didn't.

As we worked through it over the years, the lack of clarity was essentially a consequence of not taking the time to figure out what I wanted, what I liked, and what my dreams were, but instead just flowing with what others wanted, what others liked, and what helped others fulfil their dreams. Luke had his crisis of self back in his teen years, where he worked through all this stuff that I'm just getting to now. The consequence has been that his adulthood has been filled with a clearer vision, purpose, and passion.

My lack of really knowing myself showed up when it came to buying gifts for each other. If you handed me a catalogue, I could go through it and page by page, with a high level of accuracy, pick out things that I knew Luke would like. Hand the catalogue to Luke and he wouldn't be confident at all about what I would and wouldn't like.

So far, that's resulted in Luke buying me gifts like fencing classes and, my personal favourite, a pile of brochures. To be fair, it was a pile of brochures of things to do and the intention was there to follow through to do whichever one I chose. We just didn't end up doing any of them.

On another occasion, he felt confident in his initial gift purchase. He knew I liked the theatre and that it had been an important part of my life growing up. So, when our second Christmas as a married couple came along, he bought me tickets to a theatre show that fit our budget. He'd researched and researched and found just the perfect thing. When I went to pick him up on his last day of work before Christmas, I walked in to find his workmate in fits of laughter; clearly he was laughing in Luke's and my direction. He was singing a song as he laughed, 'Ukelele, me kelele, ukulele me.' It turns out that the theatre production Luke thought would be a romantic event for us—our first theatre show as a couple apart from a high school production of *Les Misérables*—was a kid's show.

The theatre Luke booked through didn't normally do refunds, but he made them all laugh so much at the mistake that they gave him his money back. I don't remember what he actually bought me that year, but the greatest gift was not making me go to that show.

As time has gone on, Luke has become better and better at predicting what I will and won't like and what I will and won't enjoy because I've been, bit by bit, figuring it out for myself.

Here's the thing: during the whole time that I'd spent trying to please others, I was inadvertently robbing myself and my future spouse of knowing who I really was. It's been a mighty mess to untangle, mainly because I left it for so long before addressing it, but bit by bit, we're getting closer and closer. In hindsight, it's coming out of that process that made me become aware of things didn't feel quite right and that I was not fully 'me' yet. Hence this whole journey towards greater joy and delight, fulfilment and purpose, fun and meaning.

In the same way that asking good-quality questions can help us identify and overcome resentments (Chapter 2), good-quality questions can also help us identify who we are with greater clarity on our journey to feeling right in our own skin.

Life Lesson: Don't over-invest in others' opinions of you or your opinion of others.

Takeaway: People-pleasing and over-investing in others' opinions of us can steer us away from understanding who we really are. Equally, holding onto a bad opinion of others holds no value in helping us discover more of who we are and what we are purposed for.

Questions:
- Are you over-investing in a bad opinion of people in your life?
- Have you made decisions recently that are based more on trying to please others than on following what you believe to be best?
- Identify a decision in your life recently that has left you feeling sure that you were making the best decision, uninfluenced by the opinion of others.

Chapter 9

LIFE WILL OFTEN CHANGE YOUR PLANS. IT WILL BE INCONVENIENT. ROLL WITH IT.

Before I had children, I remember hearing people say that it is one of those experiences that stops you from being selfish. In my nearly twelve years of parenting, I think what it does, more than anything, is teach you how to go with the flow and roll with the punches.

I feel like life for me now is having a plan A and then a bunch of contingencies based on the likelihood of any one of my children getting sick, injuring themselves, or struggling to cope.

It's not just children that can throw life out of whack, though. A new job opportunity, an unexpected health challenge, a weather event, or a global pandemic. Any number of things can swoop in at a moment's notice and throw the best-laid plans out the window.

At the end of 2018, I had had enough. We'd been doing the radio show as a business for a few years. It had been financially stressful and had put a ridiculous amount of pressure on our marriage. Luke and I were not on the same page about most things, and I just didn't want to do it anymore. We brought in someone to help us nut out what we should do and where we should go.

He asked us some great questions. From the moment the conversation started, it was a safe space where everything in life was on the table and up for keeping, cutting, or changing. In the end, we decided to go another round, but we significantly changed the way we worked together and reprioritised things in our life to get both family and work life functioning healthier. We stopped working in the evenings and on weekends, minimised the number of consulting contracts our business accepted, and deliberately created some regular family time to enhance the quality of our time together and to provide opportunities to create memories and a better routine.

Through the next year, both of us had some experiences that opened our minds to new visions of our future. Luke was pointing towards expanding into new spheres of media and, though mine was unclear, it was exciting to dream of what was possible. By the end of 2019, we had a completely different plan for the next year.

Two thousand and twenty was the year it was all set to change. We'd spoken to our boys' school about homeschooling them for a few months while we worked on the road. We had scheduled a trip to America for a conference, a trip to Japan for the Olympic Games, a trip to the Philippines with listeners for a mission trip, as well as an annual trip with people from other radio stations for a national fundraiser. In between, we were going to be road-tripping our way around the country to visit each of the communities where our radio show airs and to explore the country with our sons.

It was so exciting to pull together a new plan. The boys were keen, and I was really looking forward to having them with us for all of our travel experiences for the year. I always hate it when I travel and have to leave them behind.

Enter COVID-19. Bit by bit, we saw our plans for the year stripped away. First, the international trips were off the table. Then, the interstate. Eventually, even within our own state, it wasn't possible. Sure, we got to homeschool the boys, but not quite in the way we thought it was going to happen.

Like everyone, we had to shift our expectations of the year and rework our plans of what the year would look like.

The consequence of being ready to travel for the year is that we had stripped our business back to the bare basics. Consulting services and contracts that we'd previously prioritised were not taken and our priority was doing the radio show and our family experience. What that meant was that when other opportunities presented themselves throughout the pandemic—ones that both Luke and I would not have even entertained previously—we were available, and both took on new roles. These roles have challenged us and have actually benefitted our marriage, as we've both had independent work for the first time in a few years rather than always working together.

This has given us different experiences to talk about together.

Yet, it wasn't all smooth sailing. I've mentioned previously that I'd started working with a psychologist. During the pandemic, I emotionally and mentally fell apart and sought the help of a specialist to dig into the issues and create better thinking patterns. What it has taught me, though, is that it's okay if things don't go to plan. One way or another, things work out. Yes, they don't always go our way, but we keep going and adapt to the 'new normal'. All of us have a lifetime of experiences that show that we can adapt to change when necessary, even when things didn't work out how we wanted. We're still here and still going.

One of the more disappointing times that my plans were stifled was for a friend's fortieth birthday, a few years ago. Luke was overseas at the time of the party, so I organised for my parents to come and stay with me so they could watch the kids while I headed off to be a grown-up, party girl for the night to celebrate a dear friend. I can't even explain how excited I was. I'd bought the gift (a nice bottle of Moët), I'd set everything up at home, so they were all sorted, I'd planned my outfit and was ready with my sweet, sweet dance moves, if the opportunity presented itself. You don't always know with a fortieth if it's going to be a dancing kind of night or more of a stand-around-and-talk night or a sit-around-and-eat night. I was ready for all of it. I'd even picked a couple of my favourite stories to whip out if there were speeches opened to the floor.

When I say I was excited, it was embarrassing how over-excited I was. There's a solid chance I hadn't been out for a while.

Anyway, the day came along, I'd laid out the clothes, my make-up was out, and my parents were at my house. The gift was in the gift bag, my clutch purse was packed. I was ready for the night ahead. Come early afternoon, and I got a pang of pain in my belly. I didn't get too concerned and just headed off to the bathroom to deal with it as we humans do. Then not long after, another pang. Then another. Then another. It soon became clear that I was in no state to be heading off to a party and I resigned myself to a night of staying at home … again.

It was the best thing that I didn't go. The rest of the night was a slow descent into the depths of unwellness and all I could do was rest. I eventually caught up with my friend, gave her the gift I'd bought, and we shared some lovely time together … but it won't replace missing that night.

Life doesn't entitle us to always have every little thing work in our favour. If, on balance, more goes our way than it doesn't, we're doing pretty well. The best of life, though, is experienced by those among us who don't get rattled by unexpected changes but just stop, drop, and roll into whatever comes next.

There's no prize for the 'most resentful of unfulfilled plans' or 'biggest worrier over how things might work out'. Yet all too often, I've found myself sitting in resentment, getting the blues, or just caught up in my head trying to work out the next contingency. That mindset is just another thief of joy.

A simple shift in mindset instead welcomes joy, fulfilment, hope, and purpose. When things don't go to plan, we'll be more accepting of ourselves if we can develop a mindset that says something good will still come along and it will all work out in the end.

There's another side to rolling with the unexpected change of plans that life brings us. Sometimes, some opportunities arise and experiences that we would never have had if things had all worked out in the first instance. I was just reading a series of stories online that were talking about times when disaster was avoided because life threw a spanner in the works. Lives would have been unnecessarily lost had things worked out in the first place.

Maybe part of the trick to accepting thwarted plans is, like many things, learning to be thankful for it. If the changes of plans hadn't happened, maybe we wouldn't have met the person who said the thing that pointed us to something new that enriched our life. Or maybe we wouldn't have seen that sunset that made us feel hope when life was feeling hopeless. Or maybe we wouldn't have learnt that lesson that saved us the next time we faced a challenging situation.

These days, I tend to live life on the assumption that any plan could be thrown off course at any time. A few months ago, we were having an online meeting with our show producer, Melissa, who lives two hours away from us. We decided to organise a time for all of us to meet together face-to-face to work through how we were going to start putting the show together for the next season. We found the midpoint and decided roughly where we'd meet, and then I jumped in and threw in a contingency plan. Luke couldn't hold it in. He laughed out loud at me. Why would we possibly need a contingency plan? In my head, our producer was pregnant, it was a long drive, and if the weather was bad, I wouldn't want any of us driving in it. Needless to say, the weather was fine, and the contingency plan was completely unnecessary.

Nonetheless, I stand by it!

We don't get to control everything, and in reality, who'd want to? Find joy in the little things that go wrong along the way. They almost always become the best stories at parties as we share our 'remember that time' anecdotes. 'Remember that time when everything we thought was going to happen happened, everything went completely to plan, and there were no surprises whatsoever?' What a boring story! Life is enriched by the times it's thrown off course, even by global pandemics and bouts of diarrhea.

Life Lesson: We don't control everything, so learn to roll with the punches.

Takeaway: Learn to laugh at the things that go wrong along the way, because you can't control it all. In fact, if you try to control it all, you'll rob yourself of the great stories and lessons that come from things going wrong.

Questions:

- When was a time in your life that things went all wrong according to your plans, but good came from it?
- What are the areas of your life where it is difficult to let go of control?
- What is a change of circumstance in your life that you are thankful for?

Chapter 10:

WE LEARN A LOT FROM BOATS

When it comes to boats of differing shapes and sizes, things don't always work out for me. There are many life lessons that I have learnt from boating and most of them come from what I got wrong. As an overarching lesson in this chapter, we learn that getting in a boat with me will add an unexpected adventure to our outing.

Lesson 1

Several years ago, my mum, sister, and I decided to head off for a girls' weekend. We went to a beautiful mountain area and stayed in a lovely cabin together where we told stories, ate lovely food, and just spent time together. We were on the brink of significant life changes for our family. My sister was soon to be married and, as it turned out, I was married a few short years after that. Opportunities for just the three of us to get together, before husbands and children, were going to be hard to come by from now on.

There was a beautiful cabin amongst the trees and by a lake where we stayed, and this genius decided it would be lovely to take the opportunity to go out on the water in the little rowboat provided by the accommodation. My mum is always braver than I give her credit for, so she willingly came and jumped in the rowboat, and we proceeded to make our way across the lake.

While we were out in the middle of the lake, there was a 'plop' in the middle of the boat.

No, it hadn't sprung an unexpected leak. It had gained an unexpected passenger. A little green frog had jumped its way into the rowboat with us. Being the sensible women that we were, we, of course, simply picked the frog up and returned it safely to the water … You'd think. No! We started screaming and paddling and laughing and screaming all the way back to shore.

The moral of the story is: I don't like frogs, apparently. I also think there's a teensy tiny chance that we could have handled it better. But if we'd done that, we would never have laughed as hard as we did, and still do, when we think of how ridiculous we must have looked on the water that day. So maybe the moral of this story is that when life throws you frogs, laugh and keep paddling.

Life Lesson: When life throws you frogs, just keep paddling.

Takeaway: Don't stop moving because something happens that you don't like. They say that the fear response is fight, flight, or freeze. Once the initial fear is over, it's time to look for a plan of action to move from the situation you don't like back to a place of feeling safe again.

Lesson 2

Before I got married, I lived in a house with three women who absolutely changed my life. I learnt so much from each of them and I'll always be grateful for the time I lived with them. One day, my much more adventurous housemate, Sandra, proposed that we go on a camping trip together. We'd take our gear, get in kayaks, row across the lake we were going to, and then set up camp for the night. After camping, we'd row back. Simple!

We had to take everything with us for the trip, right down to our drinking water. It was the drinking water where things started to come undone. There were seven people, all our gear, and three kayaks. By weight, I was always super self-conscious and was clearly the heaviest of our group, so I would be in a kayak with just one other and some gear. Then, there was a second kayak with two people along with more gear, and the third kayak had three people, and amongst their gear was the drinking water.

So off we headed across the lake, but we didn't stay together the whole time. I looked back at one point and had lost sight of both the other kayaks. I didn't know if we were ahead or behind—it was a big lake and quite a way that we had to row—so they could have gone out wider than we did. We kept going and eventually made it to shore and saw other kayaks there.

Looking around, though, we realised that the rest of our group hadn't arrived. The next kayak arrived not long after, but the third one was nowhere to be seen. After a long, long wait, they eventually arrived, rightfully grumpy and wet through. With three people and the water, there was just too much weight in the kayak. They'd gone down early and none of us had gone back to help them. We weren't looking out for each other.

Despite that soggy start, the rest of the camping trip went really smoothly. It was such a fun group to be with and we enjoyed the time together. The return journey was much smoother, and we all arrived back to shore safe and well.

Just one problem. I hadn't worn sunscreen on my legs. I had it on my face and arms and chest, but not my legs. They were burnt to a crisp. Without a doubt, this was the worst sunburn I have ever had in my life. I could barely walk the next day, I was in so much pain, and ended up seeing a doctor to get a steroid cream to treat it.

Life Lesson: Always look out for your friends and keep them in sight. Also, take sun safety seriously.

Takeaway: We can't always physically be where our friends are, but to be a friend means that you are one of the people in their world looking out for their best. We humans aren't always good at asking for help when we need it, so if it's been a while since you've touched base with a significant friend, check in and remind them that someone is there for them. Also, wear sunscreen.

Lesson 3

Our next delightful boating lesson comes from another camping trip. This one was just last year. We set off as a family to a farm stay and set up camp for the weekend—just the five of us and our dog, Kosey. I knew they had a dam onsite with kayaks, but I hadn't packed swimmers. Self-consciousness has prevented me from swimming all too often, so I'd gone planning not to swim. As the weekend wore on, though, I just felt drawn to go into the water. I had some leggings that could function in the water and an older T-shirt that I figured would be fine.

I grabbed a towel and headed towards the water, joined by our eldest, Tyson. He'd been on a school camp the year before where they'd gone kayaking, and he was keen to come with me. We got to where the kayaks were. There was one man out in one already, but plenty of them were still there. We chose one each, unhooked them, and set about figuring out how to get in them from the jetty.

I went first. I decided that's what good mums do. We set an example for our children by bravely going first. I found the stairs and set the kayak in position. One leg in. One, two, three, go! Whoops—fell off over the other side. No problem, I'll just try again. Maybe I'll try bum in first this time. Okay. Bum in, one, two, three, go! I'm in, I'm going, I'm going ... I'm back in the water.

This went on for another three times before I eventually gave up and decided to help Tyson. That didn't work out too well, either, so we just went to the other end of the dam and had a swim.

Life Lesson: Not everything is for you.

Takeaway: If something isn't working, no matter how hard you try, then it might be time to look for something else that might bring you greater joy, fulfilment, and purpose. In a comparison culture, it's all too easy to try to fit our square peg into the round holes that everyone else seems to be fitting into. You were designed to not be like everyone else, so if what's working for everyone else isn't working for you, give yourself permission to be set apart and to do things a different way—to look different, have different things, and function differently. You and your way are magnificent.

Lesson 4

My final boat story comes from Nepal.

In 2019, I was thrilled to be able to travel with the Leprosy Mission to Nepal to see their work. It was phenomenal to be able to go into the hospitals and communities, meet the doctors and the patients, families, and community leaders, and hear, over and over, the difference in the work that Leprosy Mission was making.

As part of the trip, we headed to a district called Chitwan. It's a beautiful area with elephants and forest and a river and local displays of cultural heritage. One day, we decided, as a group, to head off on a local safari and then to have an experience going down the water in a canoe. We saw a few animals on the safari through the forest, the highlight being what I'm pretty sure was a rhinoceros' butt.

Later, it was time for the canoe ride. I don't know what I had in my mind when they talked about a canoe ride, but I didn't picture one giant long, skinny canoe that all of us would be in as we made our way through crocodile-infested waters.

One by one, we got onto the canoe and took our positions, which in any other circumstance would have been considered a gross invasion of space and most definitely breach social distancing standards. Nonetheless, off we went on our adventure, and sure enough, before too long, we started seeing the crocodiles. They were everywhere. We saw so many of them it was incredible. As scary as we know these animals can be, nothing was threatening about this experience. Most of them were on the edge of the water, enjoying the sunshine just as much as we were. It was incredibly relaxing and peaceful going down this river and was an enjoyable experience in every way.

As all good things do, it eventually came to an end and we pulled up to a bank to disembark one at a time. Aglow from the experience, I made my way to the front of the canoe, stepped out, caught my back foot on the canoe edge, and fell in the mud. Delicate, as always.

Life Lesson: The ride can be smooth sailing, but you can still stumble at the end.

Takeaway: In anything that you do, stay attentive right up until the moment that you're completely out of the boat. Many an athlete has come undone on the last hurdle. So, whatever you do, do it right up until the end.

Questions:
- Is there something in your life that you quit because it became difficult or there was an unexpected obstacle?
- When have you persevered even when things became difficult?
- Who are your key friends?
- What's one thing you can do to let your friends know you're watching out for them?
- Can you identify a time when you have felt like a square peg in a round hole, i.e., where you just didn't fit in?
- When have you felt confident in doing something different to those around you?
- Have you ever fallen at the last hurdle of a project in your life?
- When is a time that you felt excited to have completed a project right to the end?

Chapter 11:
TAKING CARE OF YOU

Every so often, I feel like I get a glimpse of the 'Susan' I want to be—the one that feels right in her skin and fulfilled at the end of the day, even if it doesn't all go smoothly.

Mother's Day 2020 was one of those times when I felt a 'rightness'. Let me set the scene.

By Mother's Day 2020, we'd been in COVID lockdown for a few weeks already. For me, lockdown looked like exactly the same work and household responsibilities as usual, but with the added role of supporting our boys with their home learning. Though they worked independently on their schoolwork for the most part, they didn't work unless I was present to help them sort through what they would concentrate on each day, and also, to help them transition from task to task.

Lockdown was initially exciting. Not being able to go out focused me and I launched into doing projects I didn't normally do. My first one was to sew my eldest son a new pair of shorts.

Mum had bought me a sewing machine for Christmas, but I was yet to use it. So, I bought a pattern and the material I needed and set about trying my hand as a seamstress. It took several phone calls to Mum with questions that mostly started with, 'How do you …?' In the end, by some miracle, I had a pair of grey shorts that fit my son.

On the back of that success, I bought a different pattern and started on another pair of shorts for the next son. Four times, I unstitched those things, and every time, I ended up with one leg the right way around, and one leg, inside out. I'm sure I turned that leg every way it could possibly go, and yet, every time it was wrong. This began my descent into the abyss of languishing that was the rest of the lockdown.

Bit by bit, the novelty wore off, but the responsibilities didn't let up.

The schoolwork pretty much followed the same pattern. In week one, we were making grass heads and doing art and sport, and having lots of fun. After that, week by week, things trimmed down to pretty much just doing what would meet the minimum requirements outlined by their teachers.

All around us, people were losing their jobs or starting to work from home. We'd already been working from home and the work of presenting the radio show didn't slow down. There were no days off or opportunities to catch our breath. Being our own business, we present radio six days a week, fifty-two weeks a year—though it's all pre-recorded, so we don't actually work six days a week on the show. We could create little pockets of space here and there by recording ahead, which we did, but our income from other consulting projects was immediately impacted, and so we had to be creative and work in other ways to continue to provide for the family.

As Mother's Day drew closer, Luke was looking pretty happy with himself thinking that he had Mother's Day sorted with something pretty special. Now let's just remember, Mother's Day 2020 was the one when going away was not an option, going out for a meal was not an option, and going out anywhere, except for maybe a coffee, was pretty much not an option.

He was looking so confident, though. All the normal stuff couldn't be done, so I was thinking things like maybe he's going to clean the whole house, or maybe he's going to mow the lawn, or maybe he's going to make all the decisions for the entire family for one whole day. All of those options were worthy of the smugness he was demonstrating.

Luke loves nothing more than a good surprise, but before the afternoon on the Friday before Mother's Day, he succumbed to his own amazingness and let me into the fact that I was 'going to see some weird stuff going on.'

By weird stuff, he meant things like he and my nephew walking past with our bed. There seemed to be a constant flurry of activity. Every few minutes, another boy would come running into the house either bringing something in or taking something out. It all went quiet for a long while and I realised the silence was because they'd actually gone out to the shops.

After their return, it was more activity with giggles of excitement and each of our boys using all of their self-control to not tell me what was going on, but dropping hints along the way.

This went on for a couple of hours. Anticipation was high for what might be going on next door. I tempered my excitement by sitting and watching TV while all the ruckus continued.

I couldn't tell you a thing that I watched—I was too distracted by what was to come.

Eventually, the moment arrived. They walked in the door all very proud of themselves, ready to escort me to 'my room'.

Let me tell you, all the smug confidence that Luke was emanating was completely warranted.

All of their scurryings were about creating for me a mock hotel room. It was beautiful. They had cleaned the whole granny flat. There were clean towels and a cupboard and fridge with snacks. The shopping trip they'd done was to buy a new TV to make sure I had some entertainment. The bed was made up beautifully with a lamp to create the perfect ambience.

Then there was the absolute best part of it all. Luke had set up Google Home so that I could say, 'Alexa, call room service,' and it would connect to the main house with the call being answered, every time, by one of my gorgeous sons saying, 'Room service, how can I help?'

I moved into my accommodation on Friday night and was 'booked in' until Sunday. Two whole nights with my time as my own. The weekend of solitude in 'Chateau le Granny Flat' was just what the doctor ordered. I was mentally and emotionally drained. I loved having the boys home all the time—loved it! But the pressure of work and schooling didn't let up.

After Luke and the boys settled me in, excitedly talking me through everything they'd done and letting me know all the services on offer through room service, it was finally time for me to be alone.

I sat on the bed and exhaled. My mindset was about filling the time ahead of me. What would be the best use of my time? What do I want to do and what is best for me to do?

I knew that going for a walk on the beach might not be what I felt like doing, but I knew it would be something that would leave me feeling better. So, it went on the list. There was a TV show that had just dropped a new season onto one of the streaming services, so I thought that might be fun to fill some time. I love doing crosswords, so I planned to get a book to work on.

And sleep.

Nutting that out in my head didn't take too long, so within three minutes of me being left to my own devices, I was thinking, *I hope one of the boys wants to play Othello at some point.*

We'd been playing during the week, having just rediscovered the game. It's one of those board games where I can really, really try, and the eight-year-olds could still sometimes win.

It took every bit of my will to talk myself into sticking out some alone time and trying to let it take hold. Before long, I settled in and let myself just enjoy the peace, quiet, and space that my family had gifted me to celebrate Mother's Day.

Maybe an hour later, after having a shower, getting comfy in a T-shirt and undies, and crawling under the covers to watch some TV, there was a knock on the door.

It was my Toby, the youngest of my sons, and by some incredible instinct, he had brought the game Othello over. And there it was, that feeling. I was so happy to see my son and so excited to spend time with him playing this game. It wasn't an obligation; it was just me and my son playing a game together. Before long, the other twin, Royden, arrived and we played as well. At one point, Luke came over to get mad at them for interrupting my weekend because all he wanted to do was protect my time, but I quickly explained that this was good for me and what I wanted.

I did the beach walk the next day. I did some crosswords. I used the room service to get some nice coffees and dinners and conversation across the weekend.

In the midst of it all, I found me. I'm not saying that in order to fully become Susan that I need to move into a motel and be served by my family—though I'd be happy to give it another go just to be sure.

What I did recognise is that it's not selfish or shirking responsibility to take time for that walk on the beach or to let Luke know I'm overwhelmed and just need a bit of space from the family. It's okay to just get lost in a TV series or a book. And crosswords work my mind in a way that I enjoy. Figuring out the stuff that fills my soul and makes me the mum who loves every bit of the time with my sons and the wife who wonders at her husband's generosity and ingenuity and project management ... he wrangled three boys under twelve to completely clean and to happily serve me all weekend—I mean, that's amazing!—that's the stuff that aligns me with me.

Who'd have thought that a Mother's Day, in the midst of a pandemic, would be when the penny of self-care would finally drop?!

Life Lesson: Take the time to understand what self-care looks like for you.

Takeaway: We don't always recognise when we're neglecting our needs until it's too late. We also don't always recognise what the best way to care for ourselves is, so when we experience something that refreshes our soul, releases the pressure, and brings calm and centredness back to life, it's important to take note to understand our own needs better.

Questions:
- What is something that makes you feel refreshed and centred? For example, for me, it's walking on a beach.
- When is a time that you realised you did self-care well?
- What is a simple, daily practice that helps you feel best able to face what you have to do for the day?

Chapter 12:
THE UNEXPECTED DENTIST EFFECT

There's something strange that's started happening in my life and I want to learn how to harness it. I reckon if I can make the most of these opportunities, the journey back to me might happen quicker than I expect.

The most recent of these events came through a visit to the dentist.

I understand the importance of good dental health. When I was growing up, both my sister and I had extensive orthodontic work done. I actually didn't mind going to the orthodontist. The one we went to was in Redcliffe, and we grew up in Caboolture, so it was about half an hour's drive to get there. This meant that we had at least part of a day off school, if not a whole day off, when we had appointments. My grandmother lived in Redcliffe, as well, so we'd often pair the visit to the orthodontist with a visit to 'Tapa', as we called her. At the orthodontist, I clearly remember getting moulds done and I didn't like the taste of the pink stuff that he'd make them with. I didn't like the pain of getting those braces at thirteen, either, but I did like the time with Mum, the visit with Tapa, and the drive.

Through the train-track braces, the headgear braces, the plates, and the mountain of other orthodontic visits, these all led to a strong habit of teeth-brushing, at least twice a day every day. What it didn't lead to was great flossing habits, mouth-washing, or regular dentist visits.

I'm not afraid of the dentist. I am afraid of the bill that comes at the end of visiting the dentist. The consequence of the financial fear and the up-and-down financial times that we've faced in our marriage have resulted in highly irregular dental visits by me. By highly irregular, I mean I go when I need to because I'm in pain or because something has happened to my teeth that shouldn't happen.

In March of 2010, my tongue felt something weird on my tooth. As I investigated further, I realised that a bit of my tooth was pulling away.

At this point, we'd been in Melbourne since 2006, and I had not been to the dentist, so I just looked one up and booked an appointment. I was nervous because the time I'd been to the dentist prior to that was before I got married (which was in 2003) and I'd been told then that I needed a root canal.

Nonetheless, I put on all of my 'brave' and headed off to the dentist. She started with a quick look then did a quick X-ray whilst I was in the chair. After checking the X-ray, she came back and said everything looked good; we just needed to fix this tooth with a cap of some sort. She fixed it there and then. All of this took twenty-ish minutes and cost significantly less than the shockingly high figure I'd built up in my head.

That was the last time (2010) I went to the dentist until May 2021.

One of my teeth started giving me irregular pain, and then, bit by bit over the following week, the pain became more frequent. I ignored it, but then, in a moment of weakness, I told Luke that I'd been having pain and he told me to book an appointment and go and get it fixed. He was right—I would have been mad if he'd been in pain for a week and hadn't done anything about it.

I'm in a new city since my last dentist visit, but fortunately, I have a friend who is a dentist, so it was a no-brainer to book in to see her for two significant reasons. Firstly, she's my friend and she's treated my boys—who I'm far better at taking to the dentist than myself—and I've seen her as a dentist and I know she's gentle, communicates well, and is kind. She also has two therapy dogs who can sit on your lap if you're particularly stressed about a procedure. I didn't need them this week, but I like knowing they're there, just in case.

Despite knowing her, I still arrived as a new patient, so that meant filling in the new patient form with questions like, 'How long since you've been to the dentist?' I was hoping I might get away with saying, 'A few months,' since that's how long it had been since I'd taken one of my sons to the dentist, but I didn't think she'd fall for it. I was honest and told her it had been over ten years.

The appointment went well. She knew even before she looked in my mouth what the problem was and fixed it without much fuss. The bill was, again, significantly less than I would have expected. I booked in for a proper examination, and then, we went for lunch.

Back to the strange thing that's started happening. Every now and then, I get a glimpse.

It's like a little window that shows me the next step on the path back to feeling that sense of 'rightness' in my own skin. And this time, it was because of the dentist.

In my head, I started dreaming of living without fear of the dentist bill. I saw a life where my teeth were well taken care of and visiting the dentist was part of my self-care. The picture was of a two-year journey of returning to health within my body, feeling good with energy, losing the excess weight I currently carry, fixing up the issues that currently stress me in my finances, and, what started it all, taking care of my teeth.

Somehow in the journey into wifedom and motherhood, I've thrown myself into the discard pile. Going to the dentist was part of my life before I got married, then we couldn't afford it so I just stopped going. In reality, a reprioritisation of finances would have seen me not neglect this area of my life; but it's these little decisions that gradually lead us down the rabbit warren that slowly wears away our most comfortable identity—the space where we feel most right in our body.

Somehow, a visit to the dentist showed me the path to getting Luke's and my health in order with a two-year plan, in the same way that putting on an apron showed me the path to slowing down and focusing on the moment when I'm cooking.

Having the vision is the easy bit, though. I think one of my biggest challenges is taking the next step, and then all the ones after that. Maybe what I need to do is wear an apron to the dentist and it might all come together for me?!

The next step, as I see it, is to follow those questions outlined in Chapter 1 for the 90-second change. What is the goal? What are the barriers? What are my values? What does success look like? What's the first step?

What I love about these strange moments of clarity, like the one I had at the dentist, is that the change I see doesn't happen overnight. It's one bit at a time. And I think the journey to becoming that version of me that I'm most comfortable with has to be one that happens, a bit at a time. I don't want to temporarily feel better. I've felt that. I want to feel right in my own skin, as much as possible.

My eldest son came to me recently and asked if we could watch all of the Marvel Cinematic Universe movies in chronological order. I've become an MCU fan thanks to my son who drew me into the series with one movie, then another. Then I saw *Infinity War*, and then *Captain Marvel*, and I was pretty confident that I was really into these movies. Then I took him to see *Endgame*, and I started crying when I heard the music, and I realised that I'm now, officially, a fully-fledged fan. It actually gets worse than that. On a TV show this week, they had an MCU theme and I cried—it's just becoming embarrassing now.

Anyway, back to my point. We kicked off with *Captain America: The First Avenger*. He starts as an all-too-short, all-too-skinny, all-too-unwell man with a heart of gold, desperate to serve. They give him some serum in a machine that they turn up to 100% and 'bada bing, bada boom', his body provides him with the physical strength to match the character strength that he had already demonstrated.

That magical serum and machine don't exist, as much as I'd like them to. That doesn't mean the outcome of having all the bits match up can't happen. It just means that for us mere humans without the magic serum in our lives, it takes consistency, effort, and, first things first, a clear plan.

Step 1: Get coffee …

Life Lesson: Set a plan and write it down.

Takeaway: The changes we'd like to see in our lives—whether it be health, finances, career, or relationships—are possible, but it takes deliberate planning. Set your vision, create the plan, and write it down.

Questions:
- What's something you'd like to be different in your life—e.g., health, finances, career, relationships, other?
- What's your goal?
- What are the barriers?
- What are your values?
- What does it look like when your goal is achieved?
- What's your first step?

Chapter 13:

THE COFFEE FACTOR

Maybe I've misjudged where the downfall of Susan began. I was always Susan. Through primary school, high school, and university. If I meet up with anyone who knew me back then—in the olden days—they know me as Susan. That is, except for those who call me Susie because of the radio show.

After Susan, I was Sue. After I finished university, I worked for a short time at a newsagent before heading off to India for a year. I say it was to do mission work, but looking back at it now, it really served as a gap year between university and 'the real world'. I learnt a lot during that time about working with different people from different cultures and found a resilience that I hadn't discovered in myself before. I was known as Sue while there.

When I returned, my first job was working in an office for World Vision and I was Sue for my five years there, as well.

Maybe I started losing that sense of 'right in my own skin' back in the days when Susan became Sue. It wasn't the job or the social life, though. I had a job that I found fulfilling in a team that I genuinely loved working with. And I had wonderful friends who shaped a fun, memory-making social life.

I think the downfall may have begun with the introduction of coffee.

I grew up a tea drinker. My parents are not coffee drinkers. My mum will occasionally have one at a coffee shop as a treat, but otherwise, it's tea, all-round. Tea in the morning. Tea with lunch. Tea after dinner. Tea sometimes with a bikkie. Tea after returning home from the theatre or cinema. Tea after returning home from sport or work. Tea was the drink around which my childhood was shaped. Tea sitting at the kitchen table completing my senior assignments. Tea after going for my first driving lesson. Tea after finding out I was accepted into my first preference course at university. Always tea.

I liked the smell of coffee, but I didn't like the taste.

Then, one day, a co-worker suggested I try coffee in a different way. We headed downstairs together, with her giving clear instructions along the way. Make it half-strength so it's not so bitter and overwhelming. Add some sweetness to alter the flavour. Make it a latte. I don't know why. Maybe because it sounds more posh than a flat white.

Before long, I found myself frequenting the coffee shop downstairs asking for a 'tall, half, skinny caramel latte'. And thus began my descent into the world of coffee.

Maybe all this time I've been blaming marriage and children for my loss of self when, really, coffee stole it from me.

Firstly, I dread to think how many dollars I've spent on this drink over the years. Then there are the countless ridiculously bad headaches I've had as I've tried to rid my body of the effects of the 'evil' brew that I don't want to drink anymore. So, I bowl headfirst into a coffee detox that eventually comes crashing down because, a few days later, someone I enjoy spending time with invites me out for coffee and I don't have the heart to order tea.

I let my mind wander into the realms of believing that my life would have been so much better if I'd just never had that first, sweet, satisfying coffee. Maybe it would have just been different, neither better nor worse. Regardless, it feels mighty convenient to be able to create a solid scapegoat. I much prefer the idea that coffee has robbed me of my sense of self rather than accepting responsibility for it.

If we look at this process of finding my way back to myself as a journey through the stages of grief—grief about losing my sense of self in the first place—then, the journey should look something like the five stages of grief as outlined by Elisabeth Kübler-Ross.[6]

- Denial
- Anger
- Bargaining
- Depression
- Acceptance.

Well, denial served me for a long time. 'There's no problem, I'm fine, just keep going.'

Then, anger came along. I was mad at myself. Mad at Luke. Mad at my job. Mad at life.

Everything was working against me. I was a victim, and now, I am mad.

The next two are in the wrong order. I feel like I hit depression. Life is meaningless.

Everything feels wrong. This isn't what a fulfilling life feels like. This is what being 'Susan' feels like. Woe was me. And sometimes woe is still me.

---

[6] Dr Mary Stefanazzi (2023), *Elisabeth Kübler-Ross: The 5 Stages of Grief*, viewed from <https://marystefanazzi.ie/elisabeth-kubler-ross-5-stages-of-grief>

This bit, the blaming it on the coffee, feels a little like I have a bargaining chip. I'll hand over coffee and stare down another headache-filled few days if I can get myself back at the end of it.

Coffee robbed me of me, and if I give it up, I'll find *me* again. That sounds like the simplest solution here. A few days of pain, a lifetime of gain.

By the looks of it, the track I'm on should see me feeling good again within the week. I'll hit acceptance and Susan will return to her former glory. Fist pump the air and scream, 'Yes!' into the future.

At this point, I feel like it's only fair that I make a teensy tiny confession. The whole time that I've been writing this specific chapter, I've been sitting here drinking coffee. It was a vanilla latte. It was delicious.

I realise the ridiculousness of blaming a drink on my personal identity crisis, but I do see the value in trying to pinpoint where things started to go wrong.

My coffee-drinking probably started somewhere between 2000 and 2002, I can't remember exactly. When I married in 2003, I left my job at World Vision to move to the Sunshine Coast where there was a job for Luke. Not long after, my former boss called me to offer me a role back at World Vision. The role, in reality, was perfect for me and he was generous in his offer. I think my descent into losing clarity of who I really am started with my decision to say no to this offer.

Luke had made a comment when we were engaged about feeling like he needed to be the primary income earner for us. At that time, I earned more than him. He wasn't saying that he didn't want me to work full-time. He wasn't saying that he wouldn't be okay if I earned more than him after marriage. He was just sharing this idea that he'd grown up with and was starting to challenge himself on it. I took it to heart, though, and being a people-pleaser, didn't want him to feel devalued because of what I did, so I have never in our marriage earned more than Luke. With Luke often working in missional, low-paid roles, it meant that I worked part-time to earn less than him.

Of course, at the time, I couldn't articulate all of this. It's only in hindsight that I can see my ridiculous need to make other people feel okay about themselves hit overdrive on this. I was trying to be a good wife. I just didn't see that in not allowing myself to be engaged in work that was fulfilling and productive and using the time that I had to offer, I was starting to rob myself of self-worth that ultimately diminished how good a wife I could be.

It's funny how these little moments can make such a big difference. I had some good jobs during that time. I temped at a water treatment plant and at a financial advisor's office. I worked part-time at our church. Those roles all taught me something and all had a purpose in themselves. They just didn't make the most of what I had to offer.

We receive so much value from being productive. In my experience, one of the hardest things about being in a state of depression is that it tricks you into believing that you need to stop and rest and recover and heal. Those things can be true, depending on what led to the depressive state you're in, but what I actually needed was to feel productive, to be useful, and to make a difference. All too often, I have chosen rest over productivity. I have read boredom as tiredness and have rested where I needed to work.

There's a buzz that comes from doing a job and doing it well. I have denied myself that buzz, not for the whole of our marriage, but for large chunks of it.

When I look back, I can see that I did feel fulfilled, and like me, in the time when I did go back to full-time work. After two and a half years on the Sunshine Coast, Luke was offered a job in Melbourne working for a Christian radio station. The man who offered him the job also ended up offering me a job, so we moved to Melbourne. For the first time in our marriage, both of us worked full-time—me in administration and Luke as a breakfast radio announcer.

Everything about this experience was exciting for me. The new city, setting up home, working in an office again, meeting new people, and finding a new church. Everything.

I'll be honest, though. I'm not actually great at administration. The girl who I took over from was amazing. She was so organised. Things were easy to find and clearly labelled and she was an incredible woman who seemed very 'together'. There's a solid chance that the reason I eventually ended up being moved out of administration and into the role of the on-air announcer was the fact that I actually wasn't that great at doing the organisational stuff and people eventually found me out. I'm guessing it was my online filing system that gave me away. I'll forever be grateful for the 'search' function that has saved me more times than I can remember.

Exploring all of these thoughts has been really interesting for me. I haven't allowed myself to strive for, or push for, professional success, so as not to pose a threat to Luke.

In reality, he wouldn't have felt threatened by any success I had but would have celebrated it and enjoyed it with me. I didn't give him the chance. I didn't talk with him about it; I just assumed. This is a dangerous people-pleaser technique.

Maybe coffee wasn't the start of the problem, after all. It can't be, because we moved to the coffee capital of Australia, and I sure made the most of that. Lattes all around!

Life Lesson: Be willing to do the work of finding the source of unfulfilment in life; don't just find a scapegoat.

Takeaway: When we defer to a scapegoat, rather than really facing up to the source of our problems, we deny ourselves the opportunity to truly solve the problem of why we lack fulfilment, purpose, or joy. Once we actually find the source, we can honestly and authentically address the issue to solve the problem and find greater freedom.

Questions:
- Have you created a scapegoat in your life to avoid finding the source of any lack of purpose or fulfilment?
- Can you identify a time in your life when you felt truly fulfilled, purposeful, and 'right in your skin'? What conditions existed then that allowed you to feel that way?

Chapter 14:
GIVING PERMISSION

One thing I've realised, mostly thanks to Luke pointing it out to me over and over again, is that *I am not good at giving myself permission to do things*.

Well, that's partially true. I'm great at giving myself permission to do the cleaning, or shopping, or cooking for the family. I'm not great at giving myself permission to take that weekend away, get that massage, or do whatever that thing is that is going to make life that little brighter for myself, especially if it costs something.

I'm generous in spending for my family, like if the boys need new clothes or Luke needs to get away. But when it comes to me, I tend to be more conservative. I currently own one good bra because it feels extravagant to get a second.

Bit by bit, I'm realising the extent to which this self-imposed suffering is evident in my life and I'm starting to say yes to myself.

I'm also now aware of how many of my nos are because of beliefs that I've created in my head that have no evidence to back them up. The best example of this is going to the theatre.

I grew up going to the theatre. Mum would take my sister and me into Brisbane to see musicals, ballet, plays—anything good that came to town. It was always such an exciting experience.

We'd get dressed up, sometimes even getting a new outfit. In one particularly regrettable season of my life, I would pull my hair back and curl a few strands to the side of my face to create my special look. If possible, we'd get to the theatre early and have something to eat and drink before heading inside, taking our seats, and watching whatever show was before us. We saw the works of Gilbert and Sullivan, Andrew Lloyd Webber, Cole Porter, Rodgers and Hammerstein, Stephen Sondheim, and the list goes on. All of them are wonderful memories.

After it was over, we'd head home, where we'd have a cup of tea and talk out our critiques of the show, reliving the highlights and explaining the bits that someone else had missed. I was the youngest, so it was almost always me who had missed something.

I always assumed I'd still go to the theatre when I grew up. This was a part of my life that I would never let go of. Except I did.

Luke didn't grow up going to the theatre. It wasn't a part of his story. He was open to it and liked the idea of being let into that side of my life, but financially, I just didn't prioritise it.

His first experience of going to the theatre with me was truly memorable. My mum was working at a high school and the school was putting on *Les Misérables*. Let me be clear here. This school generally had a reputation for being a rougher state school. Mum invited us to go along with her and so we did. The point of going to the theatre is to enjoy the show.

The point of going to the high school theatre is to enjoy the performance of the friends and family you have at the school. We didn't know anyone at the school apart from my mum, and she wanted to support her kids. She proudly took us all to show off the work of her students. So, a state high school performance of an edited version of *Les Misérables* was Luke's introduction to the theatre.

His attempt at joining me in my world was when he bought the tickets to *Ukelele, Mekelele* and, as you already know from Chapter 8, that didn't eventuate in us going to the theatre. It just resulted in years of laughter as we retold the story.

Along the way, we occasionally went to the theatre because of our work in radio. We made it to the opening night of *Calendar Girls*, in Melbourne, where we even attended the after-party, and met the cast over drinks. We also went to *Phantom of the Opera* for a date one time.

Then, we had children. First a boy, then two more boys. So then, I was one theatre-loving woman among a household of boys, with a father who loved footy and encouraged his sons to love the footy with him. I presumed that theatre would be a rarity, maybe a date night with Luke here or there along the way.

Enter my mum. Being uninhibited by my insecurities, Mum invited me and the children to go to the theatre to see a ballet of *Red Riding Hood*. I had my doubts, but we dressed the boys up, headed into Brisbane and, in our front-row seats, did what I didn't even consider a realistic option—we introduced my sons to the theatre. And to the delight of my soul, they enjoyed it.

On the back of that success, Luke and I took the boys to a play, *The 78-Storey Treehouse*, before Christmas in 2017.

Again, the boys sat in their seats without complaint and enjoyed the show.

Then it stopped. Until recently.

During the lockdown, Luke and I came across a performance of the song *Alexander Hamilton*. It was part of a show, *Some Good News*, that John Krasinski was doing to help make the world feel a little better during this global pandemic. I watched it, then showed Luke and he loved it. As in really, really loved it.

After a couple of months, Disney announced that they'd be releasing *Hamilton* on their streaming service. We put the date in our calendar, all set to watch the whole thing.

As soon as we were able to, after its release, we set a date night. The kids were settled and put to bed, we pulled out the wine, cheese, and crackers, turned down the lights, settled on the couch, and sat and experienced *Hamilton* together for the first time on the screen, rather than the stage. The show had always received rave reviews and we were equally impressed.

Then it happened. The announcement was made that the show would be performed in Australia. This was it. This was the moment that I could break the chains of my insecurity and try musical theatre with the whole family. The music suited Luke's style, the theatre was what I loved, and the boys were a little older now. So, we set a calendar reminder for when the presale tickets were available, and as soon as we could, jumped online and bought five tickets to see *Hamilton* live. You might be getting the picture that our calendars are important to us. Don't be misled. This is not a sign of great organisation, but a sign that our memories are not reliable and so without the calendar reminders we'd forget the things that are important to us, like buying tickets to the theatre and our children's surgeries.

The show was only being performed in Sydney, so we bought the flights, booked the accommodation—including staying with some wonderful friends for a couple of nights—and waited for the day to arrive.

What happened afterwards was not at all what I expected.

We were seeing a matinee performance and so, on the day of the show, we headed into the city early to find a place to have lunch. We sat by the water at a beautiful restaurant in Darling Harbour and enjoyed our meal together. The boys were clearly excited to go to the show, but Luke was off the charts excited. He kept going onto social media to announce the countdown before we headed in. We enjoyed our lunch and drinks and walked along the waterfront to the Sydney Lyric Theatre, arriving well in advance of the show starting. In fact, they were just getting ready to officially open the doors as we arrived.

Masks on, we entered the theatre and Luke was straight into action. He got a program, then lined up at the merchandise desk to buy some memorabilia—shot glasses and a beanie. Then, he headed over to the bar to buy some snacks and bottles of water for us all. He was a man with a plan and a man on a mission. His whole desire was to make this experience foolproof. We wouldn't be caught in intermission lines, because we already had our snacks and merchandise. We all did our toilet visits before doors opened so as to not get caught in the intermission lines. It was all about being as efficient as possible and, as far as he could control it, I was going to have a stress-free, enjoyable time at the theatre. This is why I love this man—he'll go all out crazy to protect what he sees as important to me.

The show was amazing. I was left breathless by the end of it and asked my family to let me be quiet while I sat in that feeling for as long as possible. They were incredibly supportive.

I'd predetermined what I thought my theatre life would look like. In my mind, I'd decided that I probably wasn't going to get to go to the theatre as an adult in the way I'd pictured as a child, and I hadn't given myself permission to even try. I'm so glad that I was wrong. I'm so glad that my mum opened my eyes to the possibility of taking my boys to the theatre. I'm so glad we found a show that both Luke and I loved equally for a whole raft of reasons—some the same and some different.

Now I realise that there are so many things in my life that I have needlessly denied myself. I said no in martyrdom and it's utterly ridiculous. Even if my boys hadn't enjoyed the theatre, it wouldn't have been wrong to try to show them a little something of the world that I enjoy.

So, as I work again towards becoming the Susan I want to be, it's time to take off the self-imposed blinkers and start saying yes to the needless noes of the last decades.

Life lesson: Give yourself permission to enjoy the things you enjoy. (This is actually a thing and happens to both men and women—*The Power of Permission*; see previous reference).

Takeaway: Don't live in unnecessary self-denial because you've predetermined what others will think, do, or how they'll react. Get rid of the needless noes in your life and start saying yes to what you authentically like and enjoy.

Questions:

- Is there something that you enjoy doing that you've denied yourself because you'll either have to do it alone or you don't think others enjoy it?
- What was your favourite thing to do as a child? Do you do it as an adult?
- When you were younger, what did you see your life as an adult being like? Is there anything missing from that life now that you think you'd like to bring back?

Chapter 15:

SUSAN THE MUM

In this process of *Becoming Susan*, I'm seeing the importance of intention. Maybe the reason I've lost myself along the way in life is that rather than living with intention, I've lived a lot with submission. I've submitted to the circumstances around me rather than being actively involved in creating them.

Obviously, I have created some of the circumstances. I married Luke with intention. We had children with intention, though they arrived in ways we didn't expect, like, you know, two at a time.

So, it's with that in mind that I explore what Susan the Mum looks like in my Utopian world of feeling right, fulfiled, and purposeful.

It's important for me to tackle this because I am not a natural mum. My mother-in-law described me as 'not very maternal' in one of our early meetings; and when I was one of the team leaders at youth group in my late teens, I was clearly not as gifted for it as my friends were.

My temper can be short and I'm not always very clear on what I'm supposed to say yes and no to.

I guess I should start with the things that I know. When Luke and I married, we wrote our own vows. Well, I wrote my vows and he stole them and added a line. I had a lot of trouble trying to figure out what I wanted my vows to be and so eventually I turned to the Bible, which as a Christian, is a pretty natural place to turn. Maybe I should have gone there sooner. I looked at who I could be and the words that rang out were from Galatians 5, where Paul talks about the fruit of the Spirit—'Love, joy, peace, forbearance, kindness, goodness, faithfulness, gentleness and self-control.' Gal. 5:22-23a NIV. So, that's what I based my vows on. That's what I wanted our home to look like—loving, joy-filled, peaceful, kind, good, faithful, gentle, under control, and not chaotic.

As a mum, these are also the qualities I'd like to display. I reckon I started out pretty well with these. We'd tried for four and a half years to fall pregnant before succeeding. So, when Tyson came along, I was so grateful that there was no poo too big or a scream too loud. Sure, I was tired, but I was grateful.

As the saying goes, though, 'familiarity breeds contempt'. I don't hold any contempt for my children, but I did lose patience, gentleness, and kindness, at times, along the way. My fuse shortened and my reactions were, at times, disproportionate to the act that caused them. I wasn't always in control, and so I'd later battle the guilt of having overreacted.

Some of it can be put down to tiredness, but at times, I think there's probably been some resentment in there at the freedom Luke still seems to have compared to my restriction. I can't do anything without making sure that the children are simultaneously looked after. Now I have school for six hours a day, but outside of that, I have to make sure they're either with me, or otherwise cared for, at every moment.

That's not the mindset I want to have as a mum. So, I reckon there's some work to do in this space to find that alignment with my actual values compared to my actual action.

I don't always get it wrong, though. Along the way, I've seen clear pictures of me getting it right and being the mum that I want to be.

A few months back, it was time to get new toothbrushes for the boys. They like electric toothbrushes and are keener to get in and do their tooth-brushing when they enjoy the brush they're using. So, three electric toothbrushes coming up! Problem was, they didn't have three of the same kind of brush. One came with a timer to make sure teeth were being brushed for an adequate amount of time. Another came with stickers to personalise the toothbrush. The other was just a plain electric toothbrush with a character on it. I bought them and brought them home and, after school, presented them to the boys to choose which one they wanted.

They all excitedly grabbed a brush and headed to the bathroom straight away to put them to use. A couple of minutes later, the child who had the plain brush came out in a tantrum and threw his toothbrush to the ground, breaking it and rendering it unusable.

Normal, short-fused Susie might normally have reacted at this time, telling him to clean up his mess and apologise for what he'd done. Fortunately, however, even-tempered Susan stepped in on this day, probably because we'd recently been speaking to our parenting expert on the radio show, and I do well when his advice is sitting at the top of my mind.

Let's be honest, his toothbrush was the least exciting of the three. The other two had something special and, even though he could have shared the stickers, it was disappointing to him that they weren't his.

Instead of reacting, I said, 'Go and get your swimmers on, let's go for a swim.' I left the toothbrush right where it was, put on my swimmers, and jumped in the pool waiting for him.

He came shortly after, jumped in the pool, still feeling grizzly, and said, 'What?'

I simply responded, 'Let's just have a swim together.' I grabbed whatever pool toy was nearby and we started to play. We swam, had some mock races, and made up a silly game. After a while, he came up for a cuddle and apologised for throwing his toothbrush. The apology was quickly accepted, and I simply asked, 'What do you think we need to do now?' He thought for a second and said, 'I think I need to get a toothbrush with my own money.'

We finished off our swim, went inside, and without me saying anything, he picked up the toothbrush and put it in the bin. We got a new toothbrush sorted out the next day.

This was the kind of mum I want to be. I know my kids know the right thing to do and me yelling it at them doesn't help. All I have to do as their mum is help my children learn how to change the temperature from being heated to being cool, calm, and collected. They'll get there on their own.

The same child recently started having a temper tantrum on a tennis court. We'd gone to visit my parents at their holiday unit, and the boys had immediately grabbed the tennis racquets and tennis balls on the dining table and headed down to the tennis court by the canal. It was late in the afternoon, the sun was setting, and the temperature was cooling after a warm day.

They headed onto the court and started hitting the ball to each other. Then, they decided to play some matches against each other. Then, Mr Tantrum got upset because he wasn't getting a go.

My initial, internal reaction was *I just can't deal with this right now*, ready to flare up, which would have done nothing but intensify his feelings.

With my dad watching on, the pressure of not losing it kicked in and I took alternative action. This particular son loves staring at fish. He could spend hours looking at fish. He loves fishing with Luke. Fish, fish, fish. So, I said, 'How about we go down to the jetty and see if there are any fish there?' He immediately snapped out of his tantrum and ran down to the jetty which was just a few metres away.

We looked over the edge and couldn't see any fish to start with. The water was murky and the tide low. He walked over to check the other side—nothing. Then, as he walked back, our eyes seemed to adjust, and we spotted some teensy, tiny little fish in the water. Before long, a bigger toadfish arrived on the scene, and we started following his journey in the water.

My son put his finger in the water to see if he could attract the fish. It swam towards his finger then away just before he touched it. After a while, two other toadfish came to the spot where we were looking. My son moved off the jetty over to the shore. He put his finger in the water again and one of the fish came up and nibbled at his fingernail. Satisfied, my son ran off down the waterfront and soon returned with what looked like a coconut.

Together we attacked it, smashing it on nearby concrete and pulling at the husk inside.

Eventually, we reached the nut part. We shook it to hear the liquid inside. He wasn't having a lot of luck, so I smashed it on the corner of the concrete a few times. It cracked and out poured some liquid and it smelt BAAAAAAAD.

We had such a good time together—just being present, in the moment, exploring where we were outside on a cool afternoon by the water.

As I become 'more' Susan, these glimpses of me as a mum are the bits I want to harness and they're what show me the kind of mum I want to be. The intentional mum—less reactive, more responsive, more wise, more loving, joy-filled, peaceful, patient, kind, good, faithful, gentle, and controlled (not chaotic). I know I'll make mistakes along the way, but I know where I'm heading.

Life Lesson: Be intentional in the key roles in your life. (And yes, being intentional is also a thing. Turn it to your advantage).[7]

Takeaway: We can choose how we show up in our key relationships. For me, that has meant choosing some keywords that can ring in my ears that demonstrate the kind of person I want to be.

Questions:
- What are the key roles in your life?
- What words articulate how you want to think, speak, and act in those relationships?
- When was a time when you got it right in your life when you behaved in a way that made you feel at your best in that relationship?

---

[7] PsychCentral (2021), *Intentional Living: Tips to Be Intentional in Everything You Do,* viewed from, <https://psychcentral.com/health/intentional-living>.

Chapter 16:
DOING IT ALONE, BUT NOT ALONE

The thing about bad decisions is that you often don't know it's a bad decision until after it's made.

My decision was to take a walk. A long walk. Getting the family out and about is something that we've discussed wanting to do more, but it's not something that Luke proactively leads. We want more fresh air, more adventure, more physical activity, more experiences generally, and that takes active choice—sometimes a spirit of spontaneity and sometimes preplanning.

A free Saturday was approaching, and I knew the weather was going to be good, so my suggestion was a long walk. The benefit of exercise to my wellbeing has proven itself many times, so it was motivated by my own need to get out and walk. I figured that if I dragged the family into it, then that was just the accountability I needed to actually get out and do the walk.

Two family members were willing. Luke determined that he would mow the lawn, thereby still walking, just nowhere near as far as I was proposing. Tyson, our eldest, ended up at a friend's house for a sleepover, wiggling his way out of it. That left me and the two youngest, who were ten at the time.

The plan was to leave in the early part of the morning, park the car at the north end of Main Beach, walk to Surfers Paradise, and stop for a break and a drink. We were then going to walk to Broadbeach, where we'd have lunch and a play, before heading back to Surfers Paradise for a drink and then back to the car. All in all, we were looking at around a 14-kilometre walk with three stops. There were no time constraints. It was okay if it took the whole day. What I tried to convey to the boys is that it was all about the experience.

We got ourselves ready, sunscreen on, jumped in the car, found a park, and set off on our adventure with bottles of water in a backpack. About 2 km in, the boys asked if they could stop and play. So we stopped for a bit. Toby started building a sandcastle. Royden made sand balls and threw them into the ocean. Then they started playing together, making sand balls and eventually setting up a sand ball shop. I was told each sand ball was worth twenty million dollars—a tidy profit from a play in the sand.

With about 3 km to go before our first official planned stop for a drink, I encouraged the boys to stop playing so we could get back to our walking. So, off we went again.

A few minutes later, the first complaint came. 'I don't want to do this anymore.'

My mind started racing. How much of this could I realistically take? We were 2 km from the car—that was the shortest distance remaining if the complaining continued—but that would mean no drink and no lunch. If we kept going, it was around 3 km to our first stop, and if we continued to do the whole planned walk, we were looking at around 11.5 km of complaining.

Did I have it in me?

My eventual decision was to drop the second part of the walk stop one would become the only stop. We'd eat and drink there. It would still be a solid 10-ish km walk all round and maybe the lure of fast food would be enough to motivate the complaining child to stop.

In the end, that's exactly what we did. There was one more complaint on the way to food, but after we stopped for food and drink and started heading back to the car, there was no more complaining and, in fact, we had a lot of fun walking and talking and laughing.

Here's what I learnt, though. If a walk is what I need, but the complaining is a stressor, then I need to be willing to sometimes do these things without my family.

The process of *Becoming Susan* would be so much easier if every member of my family was fantastically excited about every part of the process—exercising with me, eating well with me, having adventures, doing crosswords, having good quality together time and good quality alone time, learning together, going to the doctor and dentist together, risking together.

Unfortunately, they're all wired differently—everyone is—and we all have our own futures to build and people to become. Being wrapped up in the becoming of someone else is part of what got me into this mess. I can't now drag someone into the process of becoming me just to land them in the same place.

So, here's my revised plan. I reckon I have enough willing friends around me that I could coax them in, one by one, to the different activities that I need to do—and won't do without the accountability of someone to do it with. I could have a walking friend, a business friend, a holidaying friend, a dieting friend, an adventure friend, a crossword friend, and a dental appointment friend. Just a thought, but there's a solid chance that I'll have a better relationship with my holiday friend than my dentist appointment friend at the end of it all.

Seriously, though, when we've kind of lost ourselves along the way, this has to be something that can be corrected on our own two feet. We'll still have to do some of the stuff even if no one comes with us, but that doesn't mean we're alone. Doing things together and alone are both big parts of having ultimate success in the journey back to becoming me.

*

I've not always been good at sharing what's going on inside my head. It's how I managed to be in pain for a week before I told Luke I should see a dentist. This is the stuff where there's power in the together. It's in getting vulnerable and sharing life with people who've proven their care and investment— the ones who show up and the ones who always leave you feeling better after they've gone, even if what they had to say was tough. They're the ones to choose to be vulnerable within this stuff.

I've started to appreciate that maybe, just as we would for others, there are people in your world who would do things with you that you see as important, just because they're important to you. You just have to ask.

I recently went to an event that was attended by thousands of people. On any given psychometric test, I sit smack bang in the middle between being an extrovert and an introvert. So, on any given day, I could desperately run to people I know, hug them, and stay in their company for as long as they'd have me, or equally run out the door without them knowing I was there. Just depends on the day.

On this particular day, my general instinct was to not talk to anybody. Just go in, attend the event, and walk out the door unnoticed. We were all still wearing masks, so I figured this was going to be easy.

I walked in and immediately ran into a couple from church, Danielle and Luke. One thing led to another, and we ended up sitting together. I figured, *Okay, this is fine. They're lovely and so easy to be around, I'd be able to introvert my way through the rest of the day, no worries.* When we left each other, Danielle and I said we should catch up soon, just the two of us.

At the same time, I was sitting directly in front of someone else I knew, called Jenny. I hadn't seen her in so long, that I didn't recognise her, at first, mostly because she had a giant black mask covering half of her face. I deeply respect her, as she's wise and insightful and the gentlest leader I've ever met. She doesn't see herself as a leader, yet people are always following. So, we also had a conversation and that was left with a 'Let's catch up for coffee.'

On the screen at the event, I then saw two more women who I deeply respect and admire.

I was way up the back, and they were way down the front. I didn't have to see them at all. But that little voice spoke up and said it was time to push past the introvert in me and step out of my comfort zone. I could just say hello, that way if they didn't particularly want to see me, I could just walk away, and no harm, no foul. So, when the event was over, I went down the front and was wrapped into the arms of Jude with excitement. Jude is vibrant and curious, encouraging and wise, and leaves me looking at the world with wonder, joy, and anticipation. We left with a 'Let's catch up for coffee.'

Then, I saw Chantelle, whose embrace is always so warm and makes everything in the world okay. I'm sure Chantelle doesn't realise how much of a teacher she is. Just in sharing life, she effortlessly drops incredible, life-enhancing wisdom, and her attention alone is enough to make me feel an innate sense of value and worth in who I am. We chatted briefly because she was in mid-conversation with someone else. Our brief hello ended with—you guessed it—'Let's catch up for coffee.'

Just seeing these four women, I felt better and grateful to have such high-calibre people in my world. The next morning, I decided to text bomb them all, and by the end of the day, I had four dates set up—one dinner, one lunch, and two coffees. In one week, I sat one on one with each of these women and dragged the lessons from one to the next, to the next, to the next.

I loved that week. I had so much coffee, I think I'm still buzzing from it. What I also got from that was that glimpse of the Susan I'm becoming. The one who wants to be a friend. The one who doesn't want to leave 'Let's have coffee' as words that hang in the air, but takes the opportunity for quality one-on-one time. The one who gleans from the wisdom of others and applies it to her situation. The one who can't believe the quality of the women who will willingly say yes to a coffee with her.

The journey of *Becoming Susan* is equally done alone and together. It's just important to put the right things in the alone column and the right things in the together column. For too long, I've put things like exercise and eating right in the together column, which leaves me too much room to blame others for my weight gain and discomfort in my body. I've put the battling life in the alone column, not wanting to burden people with the internal challenges I'm facing.

Now, I see it's got to be flipped. *My health is a pursuit that only I can chase.* Though others might join me for a walk or a healthy meal, I can't only do things when others are willing to join me. And life—that's the shared pursuit. There are willing ears all around me and I am not alone.

Life Lesson: Becoming is something that is done both alone and together.

Takeaway: The priorities of our life need to be pursued whole-heartedly, even when we're by ourselves. However, we are never fully alone in our journey and a key support network is integral in helping us fulfil our purpose. It's important to be clear about what we do, even when we're alone, and what we do together.

Questions:
- What is a key goal in your life right now and who in your significant relationships do you see as best suited to help you achieve them?
- Are there things that you only do when you're with others that would benefit you to do even when you're alone?
- Do you have a 'let's get coffee' that's hanging in the air with a friend that's unfulfilled?
  When could you plan a catch-up with that friend?

Chapter 17:

WORTH THE EFFORT

It communicates a lot when you put effort into things. I understand this, yet don't often live it.

I'm more of a low-effort kinda gal.

I don't take a million photos of our children, I don't post on social media every time we do something or go somewhere, I don't make a big deal, and I don't like a fuss.

It's only now I realise that this is something I could do better at. Putting effort in—care, time, and attention— communicates so much to the person on the receiving end of that effort.

The effort that Luke put into the home motel room for Mother's Day meant as much to me as getting some rest did.

The birthday I put the most effort into was Tyson's fifth birthday party. He was in Grade 1, and as there were some nice families in the class, he seemed to have made friends quickly. We hadn't hosted a full-scale child's birthday party before with all of his friends, only small parties with our friends and family. He was obsessed with Angry Birds at the time, so this became the obvious theme of the party.

I had decorations hanging from the room and we hired a jumping castle. One of our neighbours was starting to develop her skills in face painting and offered to come and paint the faces of the children at the party. We had food sorted for the kids and, given it was going to take place in the late afternoon, we had a couple of drinks on hand for the parents.

The big part was the cake. This was where I really focused on with some care, time, and attention. Not only did I want to create an Angry Birds cake, but I wanted to make it playable. I wanted to have little pigs sitting atop Tim Tam structures, ready to be catapulted by little angry birds. There was a nest of eggs just to add to it all. The night before his birthday party was spent sitting on our lounge room floor with multiple colours of fondant, carefully crafting out pigs with their big eyes and squishy noses, and the birds with their angry eyebrows.

The party seemed to go without a hitch and the birthday boy had a great time. The best part was that it was an injury-free event, even with the jumping castle. Yay!

The effort that I had put in made it all the better from my experience, though. I knew I had done all I could to make it a special day for Tyson.

Somewhere along the way, I seem to have decided to make a day special with as little effort as possible. If there's a corner to cut, I'll find it, with a lot of statements like, 'That'll do,' until we're left with a bowl of chips on the table and a store-bought cake that says

'Congratulations' to celebrate a 7-year-old's birthday. Okay, maybe I haven't gone that far down the rabbit hole, but I have done pretty much the least I could do on many an occasion. The effort I put into Tyson's birthday party, and the joy I felt afterwards, all made me rethink things.

Take my marriage with Luke, for example. When we got married, we were as idealistic as any couple heading down the aisle. We spoke a lot about 'keeping the flame alive' and not taking each other for granted. Date night was a priority, and for the full seventeen years of our marriage, thus far, we've spoken about how important date night is.

The truth is, most of our date nights consist of us on the couch watching the same show at the same time and calling it a night. If we're in the same room at the same time, and we're somewhat without parenting responsibility, and we're outside of recording a radio show, then it pretty much qualifies as date time for us these days. It doesn't even slightly match up with both of our values on the subject, but it's become the reality of busy, parenting lives.

The difference between an awesome date night and the mini-dates we have is effort. The Susan whom I want to become puts in the effort because it's always worth it when it's going into a relationship that is valued.

Right now, Susan is thinking, *Ugh … that sounds so exhausting*, but let's just imagine that the Susan that I want to become also has energy.

Back in 2018, I was sitting on the floor of my lounge room, feeling pretty deflated. I was heavier in weight than I'd ever been and feeling just a bit hopeless about life when my phone rang.

On the other end of the phone was my sister-in-law, Lana. She rang to ask me if I'd like to join her in doing the Kokoda Challenge in Brisbane. They have a 15, a 30, and a 48-kilometre walk, raising money for the Kokoda Youth Foundation. Without thinking, I said yes. It was the end of January, and the walk was happening in early June. I asked the obvious question, 'So, is it the 15-kilometre one?'

Her reply left me a little overwhelmed. 'No', she said, 'the full 48.'

Right. So, I had four months to go from being significantly overweight and barely exercising at all to being capable of walking 48-kilometres up and down rough terrain. My head said, *Don't do it*, and out of my mouth came, 'Sure!'

There was an out, though. We had to raise money in order to participate, so I figured maybe there was a chance that I wouldn't get the money, and then I wouldn't have to do it. So, I went onto my social media and posted what we wanted to do and how much I had to raise in order to participate. It wasn't long before my friend, Kathy, jumped online and paid for the whole thing. And that was the end of my out. Now, I had to do it. I might not like Lana much for asking me to do this, but I like Kathy a lot and couldn't let her faith in me go wanting.

So, I started walking. And walking. And walking. And walking. Between when I started training and the event in June, the Gold Coast hosted the Commonwealth Games. I'd volunteered and was working at the hockey, so added in walking to and from my shifts as part of my training. I got the gear and started walking with weight on my back and, after encouragement from one of our regular guests, made sure that I incorporated a lot of hills in the training.

Three friends and I even got up at a very ungodly hour to climb a mountain together in the lead-up to the big event. I was the slowest, but we still did it.

When the day finally arrived, I felt very unprepared. I'd walked a lot. I knew I had the capacity to walk the distance, but I didn't know if I could do it at a very good pace with the types of hills we were facing. I tended to start slow and then settle into a pace. The other three girls in our team had trained together, whereas I had trained on my own.

We set off excitedly, with no turning back, setting into a pretty good rhythm together. We weren't cracking an amazing pace, but we were faster than some other teams and were having a good chat as we went. I was the slowest of our team, but they didn't seem bothered and we encouraged each other as we went.

We hit our first checkpoint feeling good. As we set off on the start of the second leg, there was a big downhill walk on rough, at times loose, gravel terrain. Things were going fine and I got down the hill okay, but a little slip with an uneven landing sent a searing sharp pain through my left knee. I knew it wasn't good, but I was determined to keep going and focused my attention on not limping. I thought that if I limped, I was just going to refer the pain to somewhere else in my body.

We kept going, hitting checkpoint after checkpoint until stopping for lunch, met by our families who were cheering us on. As we left them, we still had a long way to go. By this point, the pain in my knee was excruciating, but I was determined not to complain too much. One of our teammates had a strapped ankle from the get-go, so I could only assume she was in as much pain.

The sun was starting to go down as we hit another checkpoint, and I was in agony. We would have been a bit over 30 kilometres into the walk by this stage and were nearly the last team going. There was a physiotherapist at this stop, so I took the opportunity for him to take a quick look at my knee. He did some treatment, applied some cream, and gave me the strongest painkiller on hand. And off we went again.

Before long, we were the last team, and I was the slowest walker on the last team. Each step on my knee was agony. A lovely couple joined us—their job was to take down all the markers. They encouraged every step and paced with us, telling stories of the different challenges and runs they'd done and talking about how they got started on their fitness journeys. Eventually, it became unbearable for me and, after a conversation with one of the couples, I decided to stop. The team continued without me and completed the 48 kilometres. I made it through about 35 kilometres in the end.

It was hard to stop, but when I think back to that moment on the floor of the lounge room just four months before, what I'd achieved was no small feat. In those four months, I'd climbed a mountain with my friends, I'd supported an international sporting event with my time, and I'd walked 35 kilometres in one day with a knee that still doesn't feel right years later.

Before you ask, no I don't feel any need to go back and do it again so I can complete it. I've already proven something to myself. Maybe one day, there'll be another challenge out there that's mine to complete. For now, I've already taught myself that if I put the effort in, I can achieve things that move me from hopeless to hope-filled.

Becoming Susan is taking effort, and it will take more effort to find that sweet spot.

Life Lesson: You are worth putting effort into.

Takeaway: The times we put effort and energy into things are often the times when we get that glimpse of joy and delight, fulfilment and purpose, fun and meaning. Don't deny putting effort into your priorities.

Questions:

- When was a time that you put significant effort into something and were rewarded with a sense of fulfilment from it?
- Is there an area of your life that would benefit from you putting more effort into it? Or somewhere you are not putting in any effort, but that you think would benefit from it?
- What is something that has happened in your life recently that has reminded you of who you could become?

Chapter 18:

THE ONE I DON'T WANT TO WRITE

I don't know if every personal exploration of self has a chapter that the author doesn't want to write, but I do, and it's this one.

This is the bit where I talk about how in order to fully *Become Susan* I need to accept the roles that have clearly presented themselves as mine to do. Now don't get me wrong. I don't mean wife and mother. Yes, they're roles that are mine to do, but I'm happy to do those. In this case, it's about leadership.

I feel like I have done everything in my power in the last few years to thwart every opportunity to be a leader that has come my way. Responsibility is not something I want more of and responsibility for more people is definitely not something I want more of. I want less responsibility. I want someone to walk up to me and say, 'Here's enough money to sort you out for the rest of your life and a ticket for your dream holiday.'

I remember the occasion when I started being the person who had to stand up and speak in front of people. It was on the back of returning from a year in India. I was a returning missionary and so a couple of churches, through friends, gave me the opportunity to come and speak.

One of my first times speaking in a church that wasn't my own was a Uniting Church. It was a week when they were doing communion in the service. At this particular church, you would walk up the aisle, tear off a piece of bread, dunk it in the 'wine' (in this instance, it tasted like Ribena juice) and then head back to your seat. Being the guest speaker, I was grateful to participate in communion, so when it was time, I headed down the aisle, tore off too much bread, dunked it too deeply, then choked on it, on the way back to my seat.

After that disaster, I then had to get up and share my stories from a year in India. So, I stood up behind the lectern, opened up my Bible, and half of it fell on the floor. Welcome to the world of public speaking, Susan!

Most of my speaking has happened within the church or Christian circles. I've had some ripper moments in the midst of all of that. I've hit myself in the teeth with the microphone. I've had many a joke fall completely flat. I've turned up in clothes that I would not normally be caught out in because my good clothes were still in the wash—I'd slept through my alarm and had to grab whatever would effectively cover my body. One time I forgot half of my speech, so I just wrapped things up halfway through my talk. I consoled myself by figuring I'd given everyone an early finish.

Despite it all, my role in radio and involvement in other groups keep pushing me to the front and putting me behind a microphone.

Internally, I've fought it over and over, trying to deny that part of myself. Now, I realise the gift that it is and I am starting to love the opportunities I'm given to speak, or to emcee, or to share, or to be in the room with the extraordinary examples of others.

Part of becoming is accepting. I haven't done this well. Some of it might be cultural. Australia's 'tall poppy' culture suggests that it's not encouraged to put ourselves forward or even see ourselves as the best person for something. I don't know if it's women particularly, but certainly, the call is to humility.

Humility is important, but I don't think it should come with denial. Our gifts and our talents are meant to be used. They serve others and fulfil ourselves, and both of those things are key to living purpose-filled lives. Humility and acceptance of ourselves and our giftings can live harmoniously together and, at their best, are a perfect pairing for others and us.

In this, I accept two things. In *Becoming Susan*, I accept that there are going to be times when I'm called to lead. Also, in *Becoming Susan*, I'm probably going to do something ridiculous that prevents me from being perfect at that leading gig, like tripping up the stairs on my way to the lectern or forgetting to charge my iPad that has my notes in it and having it turn off mid-message.

Life Lesson: Accept who you truly are, even when it makes you uncomfortable.[8]

Takeaway: You're designed a certain way—with opinions, skills, talents, likes, and dislikes different from those around you. If that makes you a leader, accept it. If it makes you a teacher, accept it. If it makes you a healer in some way,

---

[8] PsychCentral (2021), *8 Ways to Accept Yourself*, viewed from, <https://psychcentral.com/lib/ways-to-accept-yourself>.

accept it. Whatever opportunities keep coming your way because of who you are, don't resent them. Accept them and accept who you actually are. It's all for a purpose.

Questions:

- Do you have a role in your life that you have denied or minimised because it makes you uncomfortable? If so, what could it look like if you fully embraced that part of you?
- What role in your life have you fully embraced and enjoyed?
- Is there a role in your life that you're doing that you think might not be yours to do?

Chapter 19:
WHAT NOW?

As I look back over my musings on where I started to lose myself and ideas on how to find my way back, I'm grateful for the journey.

Reliving experiences, attaching a new lens, and looking at parts of my life in new ways have shifted my thinking. The reality is that I'm still not 100 percent Susan. I'm still *Becoming Susan*.

What I am, though, is a bit clearer on what roads to travel to get me back to her and what little alleyways steered me off the path in the first place.

I have become aware, though, that nothing is without purpose. Though I haven't felt like myself completely these last few years, they haven't been wasted. I've grown professionally and personally. I've been surrounded by wonderful people, including my supportive husband, and my fun-loving, energetic children. I've learnt things and experienced things. I've travelled and challenged myself and had experiences I never dreamt I'd have.

The problem I'm trying to fix is about how I feel. There's a bit of a gap in the alignment of my values, dreams, actions, and energy, and it just leaves me feeling like I'm not quite myself in the midst of all the wonderment of life.

Through it all, I know that the path back to joy and delight, fulfilment and purpose, fun and meaning, is not found in guilt or shame for what is past. There's no Susan to be found in wallowing in what hasn't been.

I think, as human beings, we all have a deep desire to leave a legacy, to make an impact, and to live full, happy lives in the midst of it all. The failing of us humans is that we fall into the trap of second-guessing ourselves along the way because the way we do it doesn't look like the way others do it and, unfortunately, sometimes others can confirm that fear.

Every bit of this life is going to come and go. That can be saddening, but it is also freeing. The most significant legacies we see in our world today have been left by people who forged their own path and who weren't thwarted by the scoffing of others. They were comfortable and confident enough in their own skin to do what was theirs to do in the way that suited them to do it. So why can't I? If life is going to come and go anyway, I might as well make the most of it and feel the best I can while in it, right?

These lessons might not be your lessons to learn, and I don't think they're meant to be. I encourage you—if you're feeling a little 'not right' or you just can't put your finger on it, but you don't feel like yourself—to take the journey. Ask the tough questions. Find your source, seek out what your life has taught you, and let's keep on this journey of becoming, laughing at the missteps along the way and picking ourselves up and dusting ourselves off after every trip and fall. Let's scream and squeal our way to the end with aplomb, take the bull by the horns— for me not literally, but for you, who knows?!—and make our skin feel right around us. There's a lot of life in us yet!

My Life Lessons

- Don't let fear determine your yes and your no.
- Don't resent what you can't change and don't keep resenting the things that you can change.
- Slow down and do one thing at a time where you can.
- Sometimes the best thing to do is jump in puddles.
- You never know what you're capable of until you try.
- Enjoy the fact that people are different.
- You *can* teach an old dog new tricks.
- Don't over-invest in others' opinions of you or your opinion of others.
- We don't control everything, so learn to roll with the punches.
- When life throws you frogs, just keep paddling.
- Always look out for your friends and keep them in sight. Also, take sun safety seriously.
- Not everything is for you.
- The ride can be smooth sailing, but you can still stumble at the end.
- Take the time to understand what self-care looks like for you.
- Set a plan and write it down.
- Be willing to do the work of finding the source of unfulfillment in life; don't just find a scapegoat.
- Give yourself permission to enjoy the things you enjoy.
- Be intentional in the key roles in your life.
- Becoming is something that is done both alone and together.
- You are worth putting effort into.
- Accept who you truly are, even when it makes you uncomfortable.

Ingram Content Group UK Ltd.
Milton Keynes UK
UKHW021844140623
423431UK00014B/315